HOW CAN A JEW SPEAK OF FAITH TODAY?

BOOKS BY EUGENE B. BOROWITZ
Published by The Westminster Press
How Can a Jew Speak of Faith Today?
A New Jewish Theology in the Making

HOW
CAN A JEW
SPEAK OF FAITH
TODAY?

by Eugene B. Borowitz

THE WESTMINSTER PRESS
Philadelphia

STANDARD BOOK No. 664–20847–9

LIBRARY OF CONGRESS CATALOG CARD No. 69–10899

Published by The Westminster Press ®
Philadelphia, Pennsylvania
PRINTED IN THE UNITED STATES OF AMERICA

To
LISA   DRUCY   NAN

Preface

So little in this book is technical that I should like to begin with a few words on the academic context within which I see this effort.

There has been much discussion in recent years of what constitutes a proper method by which to do the work of theology. There has not been comparable attention to the closely related issue of holism, the total form or shape of the resulting theology. What may seem a desirable way of explaining the nature of one's faith when viewed from the aspect of methodological adequacy alone may turn out to be quite faulty when one sees the peculiar character it has given the religion as a whole. Thus in Jewish theology I object to using a Neo-Kantian or naturalist or existentialist approach because the resulting interpretations of Judaism seem to me to have distorted my continuing Jewish faith in the people of Israel, the God of Israel, and the Torah of Israel respectively. So in seeking a proper methodology by which to do Jewish theology today I have felt I had to work not only on methodological inquiries but simultaneously on the holistic question, that is to see how my emerging stance would affect the various substantive aspects of Jewish faith. In that sense, this book is the companion volume to my reflections on Jewish theological method, published under the title *A New Jewish Theology in the Making*.

I see the question of the wholeness of the final theology not only as one of the interrelatedness of the diverse affirmations of Jewish belief but also in terms of its ability to address the entire Household of Israel. Since I speak about Judaism, albeit from a non-Orthodox perspective, I am desirous of indicating what I understand to be the broad area of agreement between myself and other Jews, as well as to delineate the lesser area of our disagreements. It is also important to me that the theology be meaningful not to one class of Jews only, say the academic or the sentimental. Although theology is an interest of the erudite, what it says about believing as a Jew must ultimately be as significant to the unreflective masses who make up the bulk of the Jewish people as to its minority of sophisticated intellectuals.

The papers gathered here reflect these holistic concerns. They deal with many of the major areas of Jewish faith — internal, apologetic, and polemic. They range from academic papers to a sermon, with most of them being addressed to the thoughtful but not professionally theological reader. Since my theological interest is systematic and existential rather than historic or descriptive, I have generally not footnoted the many books and articles that lie behind my thinking. If I have any regrets at the style in which the ideas are presented here, it is that there is so little humor in this book. In many years of lecturing on theology before the most diverse groups I have found no device of greater help in communicating my meaning than humor — and the more serious the topic, the more help it is. It provides that sudden insight, that penetration to depth, that occasionally necessary distance from the material, that reminder of the humanity of the theologian which are so vital to sane belief. I sometimes think of theological wit as the Western counterpart of the Zen *koan*. Alas, what comes quite spontaneously to me in oral communication rarely appears in fitting form when I write. There are so many earnest pages in this volume that I miss the help and healing I know would have accompanied the ideas had I been speaking.

In all seriousness, however, I want to make mention of my great gratitude to Mrs. Robert Paxton, who with wisdom and

boundless energy typed and retyped this book; to the staff of The
Westminster Press for their continuing helpfulness; to the four
ladies of my household whose concern for me as I fought through
to the completion of this manuscript filled me with courage and
awe. And to Him who has again been gracious to me, I address
the words of the psalmist:

כָּלָה שְׁאֵרִי וּלְבָבִי

צוּר־לְבָבִי וְחֶלְקִי אֱלֹהִים לְעוֹלָם

> My flesh and my heart fail me
> But God will forever be my ground and my defense.

Eugene B. Borowitz

Hebrew Union College —
Jewish Institute of Religion
The New York School

Contents

Preface   7

PART I. Of Him Whose Face Cannot Be Seen

   1. *How Shall a Jew Speak of God?*   15
   2. *Auschwitz and the Death of God: A Sermon*   27
   3. *How Can We Still Hope in God?*   36

PART II. The People Covenanted to Him

   4. *Celebrating the Revelation at Sinai*   61
   5. *Who Is Israel?*   79
   6. *Judaism and the Secular State*   90
   7. *The Liturgy and Its Difficulties*   108

PART III. Speaking to the Cultural Context

   8. *The Varieties of Apologetic Strategy*   133
   9. *A Soft Word to Writers*   144
  10. *Confronting the Secular at the University*   166
  11. *Secular Conscience and Organized Religion*   180

PART IV. Judaism and Christianity

  12. *Christ-Killers No More*   197
  13. *On Theological Dialogue with Christians*   205

PART
I

OF HIM WHOSE FACE CANNOT BE SEEN

Chapter
1

HOW SHALL A JEW SPEAK OF GOD?

Judaism clearly requires a belief in God, but what variety of idea of God, what sort of mental construct or intellectual picture of him does it deem necessary? What is the Jewish idea of God?

The answer to that question would seem, at first, to be the purpose of this chapter. But I am troubled by a question that logically demands prior consideration. How can one recognize the Jewish idea of God when he finds it? Among the concepts proposed by Mordecai Kaplan, Martin Buber, Hermann Cohen, Eric Fromm, and others, how shall one judge which may properly be called Jewish? What are the criteria by which one may determine whether this formulation rather than that is truly the Jewish idea of God?

This crucial question, so far as I have been able to ascertain, has rarely been dealt with in our day, yet unless the standard of judgment about the idea of God is first made clear, unless one can establish with reasonable certainty what Judaism requires of an idea of God, the partisanship of this or that concept is equally meaningless. Hence this investigation is devoted to the question of the proper form of the idea of God in Judaism, not to the delineation of its correct content.

It will help to begin with a brief look at how some other religions have dealt with this matter.

In Christianity, it seems clear, not just belief in God but one's idea of God is crucial. This is not due simply to Christianity's early conquest and absorption of Greek philosophy. The idea of God has been of vital significance to more than Christian theologians alone. Paul made faith in the crucified and risen Christ central to Christianity. It is through a man's faith in the Christ that he becomes a Christian, that he lives as a Christian, and that he achieves salvation. However, the Christ is God, God become man, God who suffered and died, God who saves man from his sins. Not every faith will save a man. It is the specific content of his faith that determines his Christianity and his salvation for all eternity.

It is no wonder, then, that for its first five hundred years Christianity devoted a major part of its intellectual energies to defining its idea of God. The great controversies and heresies of those years all center about the precise meaning of God in Christianity. With only a small stretch of the imagination one might view all the intellectual history of Christianity as one continuing effort to define its idea of God. Intellectually, the Protestant rebellion, for example, is basically a dispute as to where the body of Christ, the indwelling presence of God in our world, is to be found: in the Roman Church, the gathered church, the church spiritual, the Spirit acting in the church, the heart of the believer, or the like.

The very term that Christianity uses for an exposition of its faith, " theology " — literally, " the science of God " — shows that for it there can be nothing of greater importance.

Because this is so emphatically true of Christianity, one should not be misled into thinking it must be true of all religions. To Theravadin Buddhism, the school of the older, more authentic Buddhist tradition, the idea of God is totally irrelevant. Its concern is the universal suffering of mankind; its goal, to overcome that suffering. The means of doing this the Buddha discovered and proclaimed. He taught the Four Noble Truths: that all is suffering; that suffering comes from desire; that when desire is ended, suffering is ended; that desire can be ended by following the Eightfold Path. As to God, however, he maintained what the

Buddhist sages have called a "noble silence." On this subject he did not speak, for as he is reported to have said about such matters, "Because this profits not, nor has to do with the fundamentals of religion, therefore I have not elucidated this."

Theravadin Buddhism has no place for the idea of God because it has no place for God himself. The Four Noble Truths were not revealed by any god. They were the product of the Buddha's own mental achievement, his inner enlightenment, as he sat under the famous bo tree at Budhgaya. The Eightfold Path does not at any step depend upon the grace, the mercy, or any other help from God. They are all acts which man by his own effort can do if he will. No wonder, then, that the Buddha could maintain a noble silence about God. Let him be there or not — it makes no difference to your escape from suffering. Let him be this or that — it does not matter in your search to find release.

And what of Judaism? Clearly, unlike Theravadin Buddhism, it has not been religiously agnostic. Jews are more like their brothers of the Mahayana school and would insist that God is indispensable to Judaism. But what place do man's ideas of Him have within the structure of Jewish belief? Is it the same place Christianity has assigned to the idea of God?

To answer this, one must confront a most difficult question. Christianity is focused upon redemption from sin just as Buddhism in both branches is devoted to release from suffering. What is it that Judaism is centered upon? The axis, the pivot of Jewish religion, is not an idea of God but the life of Torah. The root religious experience of Judaism is not escape from sin or suffering. It is the positive sense of hearing God's commandment to the people of Israel and its single selves.

Is it not Torah in this sense of the commanded life which almost all the great Jewish controversies have centered about? Not concepts of God but the interpretation of Jewish action separated the ethically sensitive prophet from the ritually centered priest, the pioneering Pharisee from the reactionary Sadducee, the law-loving Gamaliel from the antinomian Paul, the evolutionary rabbanite from the reductionist Karaite; and in our own day, it is their concepts of Torah, not their ideas of God, that separate Reform, Orthodox, and Conservative Jews.

It is to Torah, to the never-ending effort to make more precise the definition of how God would have Jews live, that the Jewish intelligence dedicated itself. Until modern times it is almost impossible to find a Jewish book whose major purpose it is to expound the idea of God. Even the works of medieval Jewish philosophy seem to deal with the idea of God rather as a prelude to their discussion of Torah, as a requirement for establishing the origin and authority of Torah, and in this way the truth of Judaism.

Nor should it be surprising to note, therefore, that it was in the area of Torah, and here alone, that Judaism chose to make exact decisions and to exercise religious discipline. The official definition of Torah was binding upon the Jew and carried behind it all the power the Jewish community could muster, from fines to whipping, from excommunication to death. The closest thing Judaism had to the authority of Christian dogma was the rigor of the halachah. The nearest thing Judaism had to the Christian creed was the accepted code of law.

But the halachah is clearly limited to questions of action, which Judaism considers primary. It does not embrace the field of thought, which in Judaism therefore is secondary. Ideas of God as such do not come within the domain of the halachah. Their place is in another realm of discourse, the realm of the *aggada*.

The halachah strives for completeness and precision. The *aggada* gives these up in advance for illumination of the partial and brief insight into the whole. The halachah insists on resolving opposing views. The *aggada* is quite tolerant of apparent contradictions and will not coerce the assent of either "a" or "non-a." The halachah labors to fix the authoritative path for all to follow. In the *aggada* the Jew is always free to seek an ever more adequate expression of the meaning of his faith. He may spend all of his life in this quest confident that except for certain minimal conditions, Judaism will not demand of him ideas he has not reached on his own or legislate him out of Israel by the adoption of an authoritative code of beliefs. Judaism has given the *aggada,* its world of ideas, an extraordinary freedom. Though the *aggada* abounds with ideas about God, one may not expect to find in Judaism one systematically integrated idea of God.

This placement of the idea of God in Judaism within the realm of the *aggada* is not a historical accident. It is, rather, a basic decision with regard to that kind of theological structure which would alone be true to the Jewish religious experience.

To have placed the idea of God in the realm of the halachah would have meant that Judaism believed the human mind as capable of reaching authoritative decisions about God as about Torah. The Torah does say of the commandment that it is neither too hard for men nor too far for them. It is not in the heaven or over the sea, but very nigh, that men may do it. The halachah, Judaism feels, is clearly within man's power to understand and extend, yet the Torah does not speak this way of God. Indeed, it emphasizes rather the opposite, that though men may know the will of God, they may not see his face and live.

Judaism purposely confines the idea of God to the realm of the *aggada* because it knows the limits of human reason in this regard. The *aggada* should not then be thought of in a negative way as only that which is not halachah. In the *aggada,* Judaism created a unique structure of thought, a special realm of discourse, complete with its own distinct standards and style, its own proper logic and language. By this ingenious mental architecture Judaism allows reason to extend itself continually, without the danger that it might overextend itself and its authority. Or to put it more positively, Judaism invented the *aggada* as the proper vehicle for Jewish religious ideas because its respect for reason did not transcend its awe of God.

Even medieval Jewish philosophy, whose language sought for something like the precision of the halachah, must be considered a branch of the *aggada,* specialized and sophisticated though it be. This emerges clearly, for each philosopher felt he had complete freedom to reject and reformulate what his predecessor had thought were the required beliefs of Judaism. And despite Maimonides' immense authority, his creed down to this day is but a voluntary addition to the service, except as it occurs in the more overtly *aggadic* form of song.

Thus in Judaism, one must conclude, all efforts to speak of God must be understood as *aggadic* speaking, and all Jewish theology must be conducted in this domain. The freedom of the *aggada*, then, makes it a contradiction in terms to speak of " the " Jewish idea of God. Judaism has only one God, but more than one idea of him.

Hence, the original decision not to speak of the content but of the form of an idea of God in Judaism has by this very investigation been justified. To have clarified here what seems to me or to someone else the essential ingredients of an idea of God with contemporary relevance would have been to substitute a Jew's view for a Jewish view of God and to strive for the authority of the halachah in an area that requires the humility of the *aggada*.

In the *aggada*, Judaism created a form of thought that anticipates in essence what modern philosophy of religion has now come to. Through the positive emphasis of Kant and Cassirer on the way in which reason necessarily shapes knowledge, and through the negative criticism of the logical positivists that propositions are meaningful only insofar as they are verifiable, a revolution has taken place in our understanding of philosophic language and meaning. Gone are the days when philosophic propositions, particularly in reference to ethical or religious issues, could be taken at face value as accurate statements of fact. Today it is generally conceded that such language is a symbolic form of speech. The significant phrases, ideas, or events around which religion centers carry their meaning in a way that cannot be taken literally or understood denotatively, but must be recognized as reaching a level of reality otherwise closed to us by pointing to something beyond themselves, in which they at the same time participate.

The most philosophic of contemporary Christian theologians, Paul Tillich, has been able to rear so lofty an intellectual structure only because he has been one of the foremost investigators of the meaning of symbolism for philosophical theology.

Jewish theology, when it is true to its historic roots and remembers that it is part of the *aggada*, can hope to find an authentic way to speak of its God. Though such *aggadic* theology is relatively free, it is not formless. Despite the many contradictory statements of the *aggada*, what Solomon Schechter so perceptively called "a complicated arrangement of theological checks and balances," it has a kind of cohesive inner structure. The masters of this form of expression, Kohler, Cohon, Moore, Schechter, and the others, have by their researches elucidated the great central tendencies, the basic drift inherent in the prodigious number of ideas in the *aggada*. These core ideas themselves, however, cannot constitute the criterion of acceptability for a Jewish idea of God. The criterion sought cannot be intellectual, for in Judaism thought, as *aggada*, is essentially free. The standards must come instead from the primary realm, that of action or life. It must, because of the centrality of Torah, be a functional criterion, not an intellectual one. In Judaism an idea of God is judged by the way it operates in the life of the individual Jew, and, by appropriate additional standards, in the life of the Jewish religious community.

For the individual Jew, first, his idea of God must be such as to make possible for him the life of Torah. It is not enough to think about Torah. The Torah must be done, continually. A fully adequate Jewish idea of God would move the Jew to fulfill the Torah by showing him the cosmic authority from which it stems and the deep significance of the acts it requires. The more completely an idea of God motivates the performance of Torah, the more acceptable to Judaism it may be said to be. The limits are reached in the opposite direction. When a Jew begins to think of God in such a way that it keeps him from fulfilling the commandments, then he may be said to have an idea which is not a permissible Jewish conception of God. That is to say, an idea of God which keeps a Jew from observing the New Year holy day or from giving to charity or the like is not a Jewish idea of God.

Reform Jews, out of courage born of conscience, have reformulated the traditional conception of Torah but have not dispensed with it. Because they believe Torah is dynamic, not static, is not to say that there is no Torah here and now. Their prayer book says, " Our lives should prove the strength of our own belief in the truths we proclaim." Hence they would agree that an idea of God which kept Jews from social action, prayer, study, and the rest of what they still know Torah is for them had moved to the border of Judaism or beyond.

If this first part of the criterion seems vague, it is because liberal Jews have kept their definition of the commanded life vague. Reform Jews do not hesitate to chide Conservative colleagues over their failure to show that Jewish law can do justice to the *agunah*, the deserted woman, but having declared that there is continual revelation, what have they done to define for Reform Jews what has been and is being revealed here and now? Just what is it that Reform Judaism feels " the Lord doth require " specifically and concretely? When liberal Judaism has fulfilled its age-old Jewish responsibility to make the Torah clear and understandable, then it will have more certain standards by which to judge God-ideas.

Yet the Torah is not meant to be carried out in isolation. It is given to a community, to a people, to Israel. A Jewish idea of God must also then imbue the Jewish mind with an assurance of the value of the continuing existence of Israel, the Jewish people.

Jewish secularists will deny that the existence of Israel has anything to do with God. It is a people like all other peoples, they will assert, and has the same biological right to life and self-expression. The logic of these theoreticians would speedily doom all Jews outside the State of Israel to sterility and decay, while it would seek to make the Jewry of the state itself just like the non-Jew. But this was not the inner logic of this people from its birth in the exodus, through the trials of the Diaspora, down to the continuing birth pangs of the emancipation era. It was Torah, not genetics, that transformed the Hebrews into Israel. It was Torah, not politics, which kept Israel alive and unified, which fashioned its distinctive character.

But why should Israel have the Torah and be a people of Torah? Because Israel felt that between it and God there was a mutual pledge, a bond, a Covenant, by virtue of which Israel became somehow his people, and he became their God. Israel exists as Israel because of its relationship with God. Whatever the Jew understands by God, it must make some kind of Covenant between that God and Israel possible; it must make Israel's continuing dedication to him reasonably significant; it must explain Israel's suffering and make it possible for the individual Jew to intertwine his destiny with that of his people. To the extent that it inspires him to be faithful to the Covenant among the congregation of Israel it is an acceptable Jewish idea of God — but let his idea of God be such that it negates the value or significance of Israel as a continuing religious community, and it moves outside the sphere of Jewish belief.

Yet one thing more his idea of God must do for the individual Jew — it must make life with God possible for him, not just as a member of Israel, but as an individual as well. Life with God — the life of piety, when we see all our experiences in the perspective of their divine dimension; the life of faith, when despite what happens to our plans and hopes we know his rule has not been broken and we are not deprived of his presence; the life of prayer, when we turn and speak to him out of the fullness of what we are and long for, knowing we shall always find his strength and inspiration. An idea of God that will not let men speak to him or let him be of help to them in meeting the varied experiences of life is not an idea for Jews. But insofar as it makes possible for them a rich and intimate relationship with God, the idea is welcome within Judaism.

The life of Torah within the congregation of Israel in the presence of the Lord — this is what a Jewish idea of God must make possible. That is the standard by which an individual Jew's idea of God is judged.

It is not difficult to see that the God implied in this standard would have the characteristics the scholars have found generally attributed to God in the *aggada*. A God whose relationship with man could be by way of Torah must be a God who cares for man, whose standards are ethical and whose nature is holiness. A God who could call a people to his service must be a God who trusts in man's powers, who is the master of history because he is its author. A God in whom man may confidently trust must be as present as He is distant, as forgiving as he is just, as revealed to the eye of faith as he is hidden to the eye of reason. Although the criterion implies a content for the Jewish idea of God, it does not legislate one. The content itself is at issue only as it affects the way the Jew lives Torah. As long as it makes this possible, its elaboration may be naïve or philosophic, simple or extensive. This is the Jew's private privilege.

Yet while one does not need to be a theologian to be a believing, practicing Jew, there are many persons for whom ideas form an important part of their lives. For them systematic thought is basic to motivation, and they feel obliged to think out their faith clearly and logically or else abandon it. It is with them that Jewish theology is born. They send their ideas from the private into the public domain, and in the process must meet new criteria. These cannot any longer be naïve and unreflective concepts and hope to endure the scrutiny of the community. They must now come forth with a maturity equal, not just to the best that Israel still contains, but to that which it still remembers.

Israel, on its part, needs such persons and their theological activity, for it is only through their ideas that its faith is made clear and manifest, subject to analysis and criticism, open to creativity and intellectual progress.

It is here that Judaism gives reason its full due. Judaism exalts reason as the corrective of unreflective faith, questioning its consistency and coherence. In the rabbinic period when the direct intervention of God through miracles to decide issues of halachah was sought, the rabbis insisted that miracles could not replace logic. In the same way, Maimonides used every philosophic means to expose the superstition of those Jews who insisted on the corporeality of God. Liberal Jews have gloried in the important role assigned to reason in their faith. Unfortunately, they have often tried to make it the whole of Judaism. Reason is significant in Judaism as the corrective of faith, but Judaism makes history the arbiter of both.

Any public idea of God in Judaism must stand not only before the test of intellectual coherence but also before the test of Jewish history as well.

No basic idea comes to Israel now as a complete surprise. Jews have a long history of *aggadic* thinking behind them in which few significant aspects of life have been omitted. Israel will always want to know how a modern concept relates to what has been thought before. As *aggada* it is free not to be a duplicate or exact derivative of the past, but it must somehow appear to be a meaningful continuation of the Jewish past or Israel will deny its Jewish relevance. This is particularly true of areas in which Judaism, challenged by rival systems of thought, filled the *aggada* with its vigorous affirmation of its own belief, as in the struggles against dualism and Gnosticism.

But here a bridge is set up between the *aggada* and the halachah. Not infrequently this reaction was sufficiently strong to pass over from the *aggada* into the halachah, and from a matter of thought it became a matter of law. Thus the *aggada* is more than a domain of formulation and criticism. It is in due course the intellectual breeding ground of the halachah. It is because *aggada* can on occasion be transmuted into halachah that the individual Jew and the community as a whole is limited in part in the freedom of their God-ideas. The experience of the Jewish past built into the practice of Torah gives them guidance and restraints. The commandments are the creed without being creedal.

The final arbiter is not past history with its literature and its law but history yet to come. The generations to be will finally decide the adequacy of a concept of God for Israel. They do so by testing it in their lives, living it for a century or more wherever history may take them, using it to face whatever it may bring. Then perhaps they will reject it as they did the idea of original sin, or accept it as they did the idea of life after death, or continue to struggle with it if they find it meaningful though incapable of resolution, as with the problem of human suffering and the justice of God.

History is the laboratory of Jewish theology.

That is why reason has never triumphed over life in this religion and why Judaism at its best has not been afraid of the freedom of the *aggada* or the discipline of the halachah. It has them yoked in a dynamic tension that keeps both alive, and it relies on the experience of history under God's guidance to bring them ever closer to the full messianic truth.

An idea of God set before Israel must then meet the criterion of history past, present, and future. It must demonstrate that it is an authentic development of the Jewish past. It must be logical enough in contemporary terms and standards to make the present generation want to live by it, and its content must be such that this life is recognizably Israel's life of Torah before God. It must also be willing to stand before the judgment of the lives of the generations yet to be. Past, present, and future; the *aggadic* freedom is given — but the responsibility is great.

Can modern Jews be satisfied with this traditional emphasis upon form rather than upon content? Can they be content with more guidance as to the search than the solution? They can if they will remember that the inquiry cannot end now, for history is not yet ended. Jewish theology will have the answer to all of its problems only on the day Elijah comes preceding the Messiah and resolves all the puzzles of Jewish law and thought. Then alone can Israel's great *aggadic* search cease, for as the prophet said, " On that day the Lord shall be One and His name shall be One."

Chapter

2

AUSCHWITZ AND THE DEATH OF GOD:
A SERMON

They say that God is dead, that we have outgrown the fright-ened, childish imagination which created him. We have heard this message for over a century now. Yet it comes to us today with new and commanding urgency, for we had been hoping in our postwar, postaffluence wisdom that church and synagogue might still speak to us.

Only now the secret is out — they have little to say, for there is no God. He died, and we must build our religion on the recog-nition that we are alone.

What shall we say to these charges, we who gather in our syna-gogues this night to stand before the God of our fathers? And to what truth shall we now pledge our lives?

Let a teen-ager decide to be a smart aleck about clothes, table manners, or his rights, particularly in the presence of guests, and we know what to do. We shut him up — or try to. Religion reacts with similar reflexes. The Roman Catholic Church may have abandoned its index of forbidden books, but the Holy Office still condemns its victims without an open trial.

Judaism has little record of heresy-hunting, but its dominant mood until recent times is best symbolized by that traditional an-swer to disturbing questions: the *frask*, the *patsch*, the slap.

There is strong temptation, then, to answer the " death of God " theologians with abuse or our equivalent of excommunication.

Yet such dogmatism is merely a shield for our insecurity, a defense against our own hidden doubts.

Faith lived with such repressed ambivalence will hardly be dependable in the face of the crises life sends us. We liberals have instead made inquiry and investigation the cornerstones of our religion, for we believe that in the very questioning itself there is positive religious virtue. Doubt keeps us honest. Last year's integrity cannot satisfy the moral demand to be true today, here and now.

So, in all honesty, we cannot *not* question — even our faith in God himself. Surely that is not blasphemy, as we liberals see it, but the oldest Jewish trait. Abraham, the son of Terah, founded "death of gods" theology, and Moses heard God define himself as:

Ehyeh asher Ehyeh. (" I shall be there as I shall be there.") We too must seek Him as he is here with us or not know him as he really is.

No Jew until quite recent times ever so changed his father's belief as to deny God altogether, yet that is the fearful possibility of our situation. If we could be certain that we shall merely alter our way of talking about the God of our tradition, we would not mind engaging in this discussion. However, we cannot know in advance that if we question, our faith will be stronger and our doubt less severe. There is genuine risk facing us, but we must find the courage to dare it, for there is no real, yet riskless, existence.

We may perhaps gain some strength from that charming old philosophical paradox which says that we cannot doubt everything. If doubt is absolute, then we must doubt doubt itself, and thus cancel out the cycle of suspicion.

We should be comforted too by the notion that our faith must always include new questions and old concerns. Not for us is the untroubled assurance of the psalmist, " But as for me, the nearness of God is my good," but rather that of his brothers, who weep and worry and wonder about God, yet trust in him. That is our kind of faith if we are to have any at all.

" Death of God " theology involves two affirmations: one about our culture, the other about truth. The one says that modern men cannot take God seriously; he is dead because he is irrelevant. The philosophers go a step farther, contending that if God is beyond us enough to be the standard of our existence, then he is beyond our saying anything sensible about him. To say that he reveals his will to us by miracle will not do, for today instead of miracles, we see nature. Where the action is, there is man, creating goodness on his own. In the face of the evils man creates, God is appallingly silent. So God is not just absent, but dead.

There is much truth here. We religious men do not believe very much, do we? We do not do very much about what we believe, do we? We do not act much different than other people, stretching to live a little better, to have more fun, to take a cruise, buy a boat, join a club, and of course — make the world a little better if we can. We have made religion more a recreation than a calling, more a leisure-time activity than the very foundation on which family and business, civic responsibility and human solidarity, rest. If religion is that trivial, is it real? If God makes no difference, is he alive?

It is in truth quite difficult to speak of God or religiosity today. We have displaced wonder and awe with the trust that everything can or will be explained by a mathematical formula. So we are no longer amazed and delighted that explanations are possible at all or that a world exists to begin with. We talk of money, goods, politics, and sex with sophistication and expertise. We are embarrassed to talk of God and feel somehow ashamed if we are caught practicing our faith.

The two phenomena — God as irrelevance, religion as a bore — are closely related, for we know that if we took God seriously, we would have to change our lives. Not that we would then don priests' robes or wear *t'filin* (phylacteries) on head and arm all day for all to see as did the rabbis of Mishnaic times. Still, looking at our very same daily routine with other eyes, weighing now the temporary and the lasting differently, seeing our goals in an

ultimate perspective, we would not be the same. We are too deeply
settled into our old, familiar habits to want to change them despite the problems they engender. Thus we prefer God dead or
merely comatose.

Yet this is where the specifically Christian aspects of this movement must be taken into account. Christians today are shocked
that God has abandoned them so long to history. That is because they expected him, on his own, to save them. They rejected
the law and placed their emphasis on faith in what the Savior
would do for them. Now as the second coming is delayed beyond
a second millennium into an unlimited future the immediate demands of interim history cannot be considered of secondary significance. Worse, it is no longer clear that numbers prove Christianity's claim to truth, for Christians are a minority faith in the
world and a decreasing proportion of the West itself. For Protestants that trauma is intensified by urbanization. The increasing
shift to large cities with their plurality of faiths and dynamic secularism has made the rural style and churchy etiquette of Protestantism seem shallow and old-fashioned.

This would have little to do with Jews had we not so assidu-
ously sought in recent generations to Protestantize ourselves. We
had been for so long outsiders to opportunity, privilege, position,
and power that when we were permitted access to them we were
willing to acculturate at almost any cost. Because we have succeeded in making ourselves almost indistinguishable participants
in the Protestant style, we now suffer with its contemporary af-
flictions.

Yet, for a change, Heine's old saw, " *wie es christelt, so jüdelt
es sich* " ("Like Christian, like Jew"), hides the truth. Jews,
heavily urban, incredibly well educated, have had a far more intimate concern with atheism in the past century than has Christianity. In Eastern Europe religion was the antithesis of progress
and modernity. For the Jew to come into the modern world, a
political solution was required, and whether the choice was socialism or Zionism or a mixture of the two, the general precondi-
tion was a rejection of God and his law. That is the foundation of

the general atheism of the State of Israel today, which still shocks many an American tourist. Yet it means that "God is dead" Judaism has been for a long time a positive possibility in the world Jewish community for us to learn from.

From these decades of experience, Jews, some Jews, have learned to make a choice. It is increasingly clear in the democracies outside the State of Israel and in some small measure there as well, that insofar as modern Jews wish to affirm their Jewishness they will do so in religious terms. They may not be very pious or observant, but they have rejected the secular option. On this level at least, they know "death of God" Judaism is a contradiction in terms.

More positively, the big surprise of the contemporary Jewish community is the visible minority who now begin to take their Judaism seriously. A sophisticated American-style Orthodoxy, to the confusion of many old-time radicals, is observable in every large city on the continent. And among Reform and Conservative Jews the single souls who are determined to know and live by their faith are no longer difficult to find. Having come through secularism and affluence, the handful who are determined to seek the ultimate answers may yet make the ultimate difference.

What the rest of us need to do, then, is to make up our minds where we stand. The "death of God" theologians are right. Our culture is becoming ever more pagan, albeit in a more elegant way than the ancients could manage. However, we Jews are securely enough a part of it now that we can afford to stop aping the majority. If religious faith is to be the odd, nonconformist thing in this civilization, then let us, with the serious-minded Catholics and Protestants, admit we wish to be God's oddballs. Every time we reaffirm our Jewish roots in study or in practice we shall announce in our distinctive way to this pagan environment that God still lives.

The far more serious challenge comes not from the secularity of the masses but from our own sense of truth. If we cannot believe in the truth of the God we serve, we shall not long dissociate ourselves from the majority for his sake.

It must be acknowledged that if God's existence depended upon human proof, then he would indeed be cold and gone. That too is more a Christian than a Jewish problem, for Judaism, classically, did not approach him in this Hellenic manner. It found God, as the Bible tells us, in Jewish history, in the reality of Israel's experience, in the mighty hand and outstretched arm which alone explained its genesis, its exodus, its laws, and its leaders. For millennia through Biblical and Talmudic times, the Jews celebrated festival by festival their great historic encounters with God, and from the calendar by which they regulated their lives learned to interpret their present changing fortunes. They knew God because they were Jews — it was as simple and unphilosophic as that. Only when Jews entered a culture, such as that in Alexandria, Spain, or Germany, where Greek philosophy thrived, did they learn its current modes and use them to explain their Judaism. When they were not in such cultures, they had no need of anything other than the reality conveyed by authentic Jewish living.

That is our difficulty. We no longer know integrated Jewish being. We are split personalities, persons who are also Jewish, human beings who happen to share in Jewish faith. We are affected by the " death of God " discussion because we are no longer so fundamentally at home in our Jewish reality that we know God from our very own existence. So we are now condemned to regain him through the modern sense of truth and value that we share. Yet what if the secular way modern man thinks inevitably bars the possibility of there being a God? Then we must ascertain how it knows that this is the one and only way to know the truth, a way so certain that it may stand up to God himself and say, " Unless you meet our standards you cannot exist! " We are compelled to make that inquiry of dogmatic empiricism or scientism because we know from our own immediate experience that we are more than all the scientific data that can ever be compiled about us. We are more than chemical exchanges, psychic dynamisms, and social patterns. We know ourselves to be persons — single, unique, irreplaceable — and there is no reality of which we can be more certain than of ourselves. The most real things to persons, the ones by which we judge our lives to be full or empty — love, loyalty, courage, hope — regularly call us to go beyond evidence or our powers of description. He who cannot face the risk of such commitment cannot ever be a person. He moves among us, but because his model is a machine, as a person he is dead.

That is why Jews have not, on the whole, been deeply moved by the metaphysical or linguistic discusssions of the " death of God " theologians. Jews have always known in their commitment to *mitzvah* over dogma that we cannot ever adequately talk about God, though we can hope to live according to his will. Is there a Jew so ignorant that he does not know the most common Jewish rule concerning God? We know him by his very own name, but we may not utter it.

So the Jewish concern with the death of God differs from that which is trumpeted in the press. The Jews have known God from their history, but what shall we say of his presence in Jewish history in recent years? Where was he when Hitler did what no man should ever do? Why did He not reveal himself to a supplicating, forsaken people who might have died in triumph if only they could have been certain that they died in his name? And why does he keep silent now when we the guilty survivors of that fearful generation beg for a glimmer of understanding and a particle of assurance that we may live so as to make their deaths meaningful?

God's absence in the real affairs of men then and now — that is the Jewish version of the death of God. To those who lost their faith along with their loved ones, we do not try to give explanations but falteringly hold out the helping hand of common humanhood and the open heart of compassionate concern. In the face of their loss what can man say?

But it cannot end there. We who can find the strength, the courage, to stay Jews must not let it end there, for if God is dead, then Auschwitz was not despicable and Treblinka was permitted. If there is no transcendent standard of holiness by which all men are bound, then why should the strong not rule and torture and destroy? If God is dead, then, as Ivan Karamazov said, then all things are possible. We twentieth-century men have proved in practice what that might mean, but the Jewish people knows that history is more than the house of bondage. We came into being as a people in Egypt and pledged ourselves to God at Sinai, so that the message of redemption, dim and obscure as it may be in one era or another, will never be forgotten among men. As long as we are in history, faithful to him, men cannot ignore God. That is why they hate and have sought to destroy us. We are God's hostages in history. Shall we now abandon him and reject this historic role? By denying him and thus admitting the legitimacy of every viciousness, do we hope to be more honest to ourselves — when honesty itself will no longer be a virtue? And what will our abandonment make of the six million? We do not know, we cannot understand, how God could permit such evil — but we cannot deny that we know what in all duty and responsibility we now must do.

Each time we do a Jewish act, perform a Jewish command, participate in a Jewish endeavor, affirm such Jewish faith as we can muster, we signify that we shall not let God die in history. He may be withdrawn, but we shall remain here to affirm his being; he may be absent, but we shall stand here for his presence; he may be eclipsed, but we shall stiff-neckedly wait here for his emergence. We shall not let him go. For the sake of our fathers, for the sake of our children, for the sake of our martyrs — we shall not let him go.

Whence comes the courage for such assertion against men at their worst and God at his most difficult? We do not know. Yet we know it is as an old and cherished Jewish gift, and we know it bears a strength beyond our own. Perhaps defiance will be the means by which we learn how real and present is the Lord our God.

O God, we beseech thee,
Find us as we seek to find our way to thee, for we are small
of strength and weak of will.

Try us not, O Lord, with the great tests for we yearn not to fail thee and our brothers.

Be satisfied, O God, to prove us with the trials of the day to day, the ordeals of the ordinary, for we are not as brave as we would wish to be, nor as strong as thou dost require.

Forgive us, Lord, for having failed thee again and again, and grant unto us the courage to testify of thee in all our ways. Amen.

Chapter

3

HOW CAN WE STILL HOPE IN GOD?

The work of Jewish theology today, as I understand it, must be carried out from a postsecular stance. Because that position determines the view of hope offered here, some preliminary remarks concerning it are required.

With the emancipation of the Jews from ghetto existence beginning about the end of the eighteenth century, Judaism underwent a steady process of secularization in the contemporary, limited sense of that term. On one level that was associated with the radical change in the political status of the Jews. Only with the emergence of a secular as contrasted to a Christian state was it possible for Jews to have full rights as citizens. The Jews therefore welcomed the secular state in Western Europe and avidly took advantage of its new opportunities for civic participation. That implied the acceptance of a certain neutral, religion-free area of existence, and this basic political secularization was amplified by the urban concentration of Jews and their speedy movement into the universities wherever this was permitted. As the nineteenth century proceeded this process moved toward self-consciousness. Traditional Judaism saw the need to explain itself to the surrounding world, or what is the same, having adopted the style of the general society, it now had to explain itself to itself in society's terms. That meant using the language of secular philosophy to talk about Judaism, and although German idealism was more hospitable to religious interpretation than contemporary secular philosophy is, the very process of employing a philosophic hermeneutic made its demands for the transformation of Judaism. These social and intellectual pressures were so great that when Orthodox Judaism emerged in the person of Samson Raphael Hirsch, it as well as Reform Judaism appeared as a self-consciously " religious " movement and thus, as contrasted to the older synthesis of folk and faith, one touched by the modern secular spirit. The effects were internal as well. Among the Reform Jews the service was translated into the vernacular, the legal disciplines were reduced to subjective desirables, and the clergy lost its aura of infallibility. Yet even among the traditionalists the observance of Jewish civil law speedily gave way to the use of the government's courts and general as well as Jewish education became acceptable, both unthinkable concepts a century before. The decades have only increased this involvement with secularity.

The process took a more radical turn on the part of those Jews who felt that modernity meant some sort of scientific or materialistic positivism. By the last quarter of the nineteenth century many Jewish intellectuals knew God was dead and religion was hopelessly outmoded. They wrote about it, preached it, and organized in terms of it. Their substitutes for Jewish faith, which were very much felt in the Jewish world, took the form of socialism if they were determined to transcend their Jewishness, or Zionist nationalism if they were proud of it, or socialist Zionism if they wanted the best of both worlds. They demythologized Jewish religious concepts into politics. The prophets were early agitators for social justice. *Galut*, " exile," was a matter of political geography rather than equally the metaphysical alienation of God and man in this world. *G'ulah*, " redemption," they took back to its early sense of reacquiring one's family land instead of equally meaning the establishing of the Messianic Kingdom. The State of Israel is the fulfillment of that secularization of Judaism.

In the United States these European activities came much later, mass migration being a late nineteenth- early twentieth-century

phenomenon, and were transformed by the special social situation
of an open and expanding society. Its early and perhaps characteristic example was the establishment of the Ethical Culture Movement by a Jew, and the large number of Jews who once flocked
to it as a perfect synthesis of the nonsacred in Judaism with the
moral in democracy. Today it would seem that the high point
of American Jewish secularization was reached just before World
War II. There were by then enough native-born Jews and aspir-
ing young immigrants in the universities or involved in the general, secular culture for them to have a positive intellectual in-
ducement to give up their ancestral religion. What gave that
movement tremendous force in the Jewish community was its
linkage to the psychosocial pressures generated by the cultural
distance between the immigrant Yiddish-speaking elder generation and their American-oriented children. So, for Jewish youth,
Americanization meant nonobservance of Jewish law, sophistication meant atheism. Statistically, these may not have determined
the majority style, yet they were widespread, well known and
much worried over. No wonder that spokesmen for Judaism in this
period were seeking secular syntheses by elaborating a naturalist,
that is, functional nonmetaphysical, explanation of Jewish faith,
as was Mordecai Kaplan, or experimenting with other even less
God-oriented forms of humanism.

Anyone who has lived through these past few decades of American Jewish history or who has because of his own struggle made
vicariously his own the difficulties of the Jewish community in the
century and a half since the emancipation began — and it is not
yet nearly complete — cannot help marveling at the revolution
that the discovery of the secular realm has apparently begun in
both Protestant and Catholic circles. We always thought the
church was in the world and part of the culture while we were still
emerging. Now we wonder what kind of spiritual ghetto Christianity seeks emancipation from. Usually, Jews borrow theological
patterns from their neighbors. For a change, a theological movement seems to have passed through Judaism before reaching Christianity, almost certainly because we are structured as a folk or a

people and not as a church. We could not, therefore, even in pre-emancipation days, be as separate from the secular as Christians have felt themselves to be.

From these decades of experience with secularity it is partly sad and partly astonishing to hear secularity being welcomed today as a religious aid of messianic proportions. Of course one must understand and in part accommodate himself to contemporary secularity. One must speak to modern man in a modern way. However, the Jewish experience is that translating the service not only makes it understandable but also unbelievable to many; turning law into a matter of individual decision leads not only to willing compliance but to gross nonobservance, almost to anarchy; and humanizing the authorities makes them not only more approachable but less influential in most people's lives. A religious concern with the secular style of our time may solve some of our older pressing problems and so may be necessary, but it will also negate many of the old values that religion has treasured and create new problems which will then demand newer solutions. This is what brings Jews to a postsecular stance.

Since World War II the Jewish community seems to have rounded a theological corner, at least in some small minority of its members. I do not refer now to the unexpectedly high proportion of Jews who affiliate with synagogues, who have built an incredibly large number of beautiful religious centers, and who in some measure participate in their activities. Although no observer of American Jewish life in the late thirties could have expected it, such a return today seems more often a new way of secularizing Judaism than a genuine religious movement. What is even more unexpected and important is that small group who, having come through atheism or socialism or ideological Zionism or pure secularist indifference, are now seriously seeking the meaning of Jewish faith. On the intellectual level it is an interdenominational — *mirabile dictu* — group of theologians and rabbis who are trying to go beyond Buber and Rosenzweig in the search of a new sense of Covenant, law, and community. They find themselves met in every Jewish community they visit by a small but thoughtful band

who are anxious to hear about Jewish belief, and the more existentially challenging the presentation the better. They are not
many but that they exist at all, that they care as they do, is what
provides the social reality of this postsecular stance of Jewish theology. In concern if not yet in theological substance they know
why they are Jewish. By contrast why should one who takes secularity seriously care about his Jewishness? Ethics are universal;
psychic needs are for experiences to fill or doctors to treat; belong-
ing is supplied by Americanism; ethnic enrichment, by folk music
or crafts imported from the whole world; culture is forced on us
all by a booming culture industry. So a large number of Jews are
too secular to take Judaism or even Jewishness seriously, yet have
too much self-respect to surrender them entirely. That is what the
alliance with secularity has brought Jews to and that is why, living
with it for years now, I approach the analysis of modern man's
sense of hope in the future not uncritically.

There can be little doubt that all of us today are very much
concerned with what is new, with what is coming to be. On a vulgar level much of our economy is based on it. The annual change
in automobile models sets a tone that appliance, clothes, and other
manufacturers seek to emulate. Imagine, we engineer for obso-
lescence! We are equally concerned with the novel in our social
styles, looking for the new restaurant, resort, or the thing to do.
Our omnipresent communications media put their great energy
into what they know will sell, the sensational and the different.

That is the superficial side of what technology and history have
taught us. Invention has demonstrated again and again that things
need not be what they were. Looking back over the ages, we find
that the men most admired are the innovators who have improved man's condition or broadened the horizons of his spirit.
Those movements have not stopped. That good future we would
like is even now coming into being. Today is even now becoming
" the old days."

There is much in this modern mood about which religion and
the contemporary secular spirit can agree. Both are discontent
with the present situation of man and society. They know things

are not what they ought to be and that it is critical for man to devote himself to making them better. Secular man proposes to do so by what we may call horizontal transcendence. By projecting human creativity forward through time he hopes to overcome the present problems. There is in all logical rigor no present evidence that such a positive outcome is possible. All we can see are difficulties, false solutions, and creative discontent. We do have some experience of having met such problems in the past. Still, that says nothing in principle about these problems. Even in secular hope, however, there is also a certain measure of faith, a commitment that goes beyond the present evidence and is strong enough to build one's life upon.

Here, too, religious men and those of a secular temper can meet, for this horizontal conception of hope is clearly to be seen in the Bible. The major Hebrew term for " hope," *k-v-h*, means in the Bible not just a state of soul but an expectation in time. The dictionaries often give its meaning as " to wait for." Hope in God is the trust a man has, in his present distress, that God will soon act to bring him relief. That temporal sense of hope is reinforced by the frequent parallelism of terms from the root *k-v-h* with those from *y-h-l*, which far more specifically means " to wait " or " to look for." Another root similarly but less frequently used in these contexts, *h-k-h*, even more concretely denotes temporal expectation. Much has been written about the historical orientation of Biblical faith, and this is surely a striking corroboration of it. Our most natural inclination today would be to think of hope as something inner, emotional, essentially subjective, yet for the Bible it is quite objectively connected with events that are to take place in time. Moreover, where we would assume that hope was primarily for the self or perhaps for a man's loved ones, it is in the Bible as much a concern for the community, the people of Israel, as it is for the individual. When the Hebrews express their folk distress and hope in God, they say they wait for him, which means that they await the time when he will make himself felt in history on their behalf. That sense of communal hope is one of the most common prophetic and psalmic themes. And the individual and corporate levels do not contradict each other. Rather, they seem to be complementary. Thus very often it is difficult to tell in the psalms whether the usage, though expressed individually, is not meant communally. On occasion a clear-cut community usage suddenly slips into the first person or vice versa. In Biblical times, the individual and the people were not nearly so separate as they are today when subjective autonomy and individualism are methodological necessities. In ancient times, self and folk merged, the one into the other.

That may help make clear why even personally there was such a strong sense of temporal hope in Biblical Judaism. The major historic event it knew and celebrated was the exodus from Egypt. That experience of God's helping power seems to have been as dominant a motif of Jewish faith as anything one can find in the Biblical experience. God had brought the people forth from slavery and given them a law and a land. He became the Hebrews' God by overcoming a tragic historic situation and turning it into one of fulfillment. Regardless of how many tribes actually participated in it, the exodus became the major religious memory of all the people of Israel, and their hope was that God would again and again save them in history. The individual Hebrew, one may surmise, by participating in his people's sense of having a God who saved, came to understand the experience of his own life in similar bondage-transcending, exodus-granting terms. He, too, could hope that God would act on his behalf in the situation in which he found himself. Both levels of expectation — that the people and the individual alike would find God working on their behalf to bring them out of their trouble — were confirmed by their experience. God did help them often. This does not mean that God always gave them prosperity and success. They had the capacity to see him working for their benefit even in what otherwise would have appeared as defeat or disaster. Perhaps that is why they did not lose their faith in his active presence in history when it might seem that he had deserted them. Their trust that he would yet act, for individuals and community alike, was often strained and they expressed their feelings to their God in terms of desperation. Yet it held fast through centuries of trial and then every new Exodus-experience now made the old Egyptian events the faithful paradigm of God's living, active relationship with his people and each of its members.

That sense of God's present power in history is a major ingredient in the Hebrew understanding that the relationship with God is best symbolized by the concept "Covenant." God's responsibility in that relationship is, among other things, to save his people. One might then say that because Israel has a Covenant with God, it can hope that he will act for them in history. That describes it in fairly clear Biblical terms, though I think the religious reality is better put this way: because the people of Israel knew that God worked on their behalf in history, they could use the juridic concept "Covenant" to symbolize their relationship with him.

What is critical from the point of view of the modern theological problematic is the dialectic sense of action under the Covenant. Because God is expected to act does not mean that man may now do nothing and simply wait. The Hebrews must walk themselves out of Egypt, though they know they were borne on eagles' wings. The Hebrew Judges and kings must lead their armies into battle, even though they have been told that the Lord will fight for them. To be sure, God occasionally takes quite independent action in the form of a miracle. That is his free right as sovereign Lord. Yet the law forbids testing him in this regard, and waiting for his help therefore does not mean giving up trust in what men must yet do. Only when everything has been done does one wait for a miracle.

The human side of the Covenant dialectic of action is, as befits man's stature in contrast to God's, far more limited. For man simply to act on his own, that is to say, without regard for his Covenant partner, is always wrong. It may seem to lead to success but it is nonetheless sin and will be met with punishment. Man's action is truly significant only when it takes place in accordance with God's will. Since he is sovereign in history such acts can endure and bring blessing. More, when a man does them, he knows he does them with God's help, for that is the direction in which God himself is moving history. The act is now quite precisely a Covenant act in which man and God join together to do a deed, yet each remains himself in his own integrity. On the common, everyday level, Jewish hope is the hope that God is joining in what men are doing, that they are doing acts in which God can participate. That sense of Covenant partnership in the deeds of the everyday is in principle no different from its more dramatic manifestation in moments of danger, personal or communal, when the faithful trust that God will act on their behalf. The pious, however, have always realized that this was equally true of every act men did in calmer and more quiet days.

This Covenant dialectic of God and man linked to one another in any meaningful historical activity is to be found almost everywhere in the Bible. Eventually and inevitably, so it would seem, it leads on to a third level of hope, that God will use his saving power in such a way that there will be, so to speak, no more need for him to act again. One day there will be an entrance into the promised land of God's rule and man's full-hearted obedience. That dream of Hebrew eschatology is quite difficult to trace in its genesis and historical development. Shall the prophetic symbols for the age to come be taken rather literally to counteract the unwarranted spiritualization of the prophetic writings by generations of homileticians, or shall they be understood in symbolic depth, using the human language of a given time and place to express a truth that here as elsewhere transcends its environment? Shall one say that the prophets before the exile spoke only of doom and not of hope, or if reproof without hope seems unreasonable, then how much hope may an early voice be permitted to have in a non-Hegelian world? And how shall one determine the criteria by which he chooses the criteria by which to give his answers?

What can safely be said in the face of these problems is that Biblical Judaism came eventually to contain an eschatological level in its hope which seems perfectly in keeping with its sense of the Covenant between God and Israel. If God is truly sovereign over the creation and concerned that his will be done among men, if he repeatedly acts to make this happen and covenants with Israel to bring it about, then it seems reasonable that in due course he should see to it that this effort reaches a proper conclusion. That alone is commensurate with his sole rule as God. It also reinforces and is in turn strengthened by the individual and folk levels of Biblical faith. Every saving act on the personal or communal level substantiated the faith that God's Kingdom would one day come on earth. When the individual or the people of Israel verged on despair, they were buoyed by the knowledge that any defeat they might now suffer could not impede God's and therefore Israel's ultimate triumph in history.

Jews have always been incredulous when they have been told that Israel's Covenant and its eschatological hope are contradictory, that only by its Covenant being broken or superseded could its messianic visions be fulfilled. Jews today remain no less convinced. If anything, they are somewhat astonished that so archaic an attitude, so pre-Conciliar a point of view can still be heard in serious scholarly circles. Were the exilic and postexilic prophets of the Bible not truly God's prophets when they called for the reestablishment of the Temple and the observance of Jewish law, and affirmed the eternity of Israel's relationship to God? Was the Jewish people which heard the prophets and preserved their writings and transmitted their message in unbroken tradition over the centuries completely misled and deluded? Even more important, was the community of Israel throughout the ages, indeed, is the Household of Israel today, God's people, not as truly bound to him in a Covenant as real and as effective today as when it was made at Sinai? Any imputation that there can be no living religious reality to Israel's presence in the world today or that there cannot be any integrity to its structure of hope must be rejected by Jews as blindness to the reality of Biblical faith and its living manifestations in Jewish lives today as well as throughout the ages.

Regardless of the origins of Jewish eschatology, it was by the early centuries of the Common Era as fundamental to Jewish hope as was God's trustworthiness toward individuals and the peo-

ple as a whole. It is true that some rabbis speak of the Messianic
Era in quite naturalistic terms while others give a miraculous interpretation. Often that spectrum of opinion exists because of a
distinction between a naturalistic messianic time which is only
the prelude to the transnaturalistic Kingdom of God himself,
though this usage is not fully consistent. The rabbis did not encourage such antihistorical speculation, yet allowed great individual freedom in formulating those speculations which did arise.
They could do so because they firmly fixed eschatological as well
as personal and communal hope into the pattern of Jewish observance. Thus in the required worship, hope is a leading motif
of the *kaddish* doxology, is found in four of the last five of the
regular petitions of the daily service, and is the major theme of
the New Year's and Day of Atonement liturgy. Indeed, the place
where the word " hope " figures most prominently in Jewish liturgy
is the original New Year's prayer for the establishment of God's
Kingdom, which for about the past six centuries has closed every
Jewish service. Its second paragraph begins, " We therefore hope
in Thee, O Lord our God, that we may speedily behold the glory
of Thy might, when Thou shalt remove idols from the earth and
the non-gods shall be utterly destroyed, when Thou shalt establish
the world as The Kingdom of God." One can also see the eschatological dimension of Jewish hope intertwined with the individual and folk concerns in the opening paragraph of the petitions
recited at least three times each day. The mighty God who yet
helped one man, Abraham, is now addressed as he who will bring
a redeemer to save all the Household of Israel.

This brief survey should be sufficient to indicate why that old
Jewish hope is unacceptable to modern secular man. Though Biblical Judaism too knows dissatisfaction with the present and has
faith that it will be transcended in time to come, it affirms this
horizontal trust because it knows a vertical reality. It believes the
present can be transcended because it believes in a transcendent
God. There the paths diverge. Secular man, by popular definition,
knows no transcendent reality. His hope for the future is in the
enhancement of man's capabilities. With the improved techniques

and knowledge that time will bring, man will be able to overcome problems which are not now soluble. That represents only
faith in man and his capacities, perhaps too a trust in nature's
accommodation to man or a sense that to change things may
therefore change the quality of existence. All these factors may
still be called horizontal.

That is what makes Marxism such an interesting case in the
contemporary secular world. At one time a Marxist view of society and history might well seem to qualify as the height of secularity. Today's secularity is too radical for such a judgment. Marxism still bears the genetic signs of its idealistic parentage, for it
retains a sense of transcendence even though it has sought to
stand the Hegelian dialectic on materialistic feet. The classic
Marxist believes that there is at work in and through history a
process which will inevitably bring about the socialist state or
some other such messianic surrogate. It would be wisest for men
to identify and cooperate with this inevitable development, but
even if they do not, it will surely come to be. What powers this
hope is its recognition of a process beyond man's ultimate control
that moves history to a predetermined end. It may be located in
nature and closely identified with economic structures and dy-
namics, but insofar as it is beyond deflection or control it is in
the category of transcendent realities. Moreover, since it is in-
accessible to test or verification, yet explains everything, it seems
in Marx's own sense an ideology, and a religious one at that. There
may be great virtue in creating dialogues with Marxists today, particularly in Europe, yet that has little to do with the problem of
interpreting religion to secular man. Because he rejects all transcendence and ideological formulation for his tentative commitments and pragmatic understandings, he is essentially post-Marxist
with regard to history even where he uses Marx's sociology, and
that seems increasingly true in Europe as in the United States.
Indeed, one cannot help wondering if it is not a recognition of its
failing intellectual appeal that makes Marxism open to discussion
with religion.

The fundamental question, then, between secularists and Biblical religion is, To what extent is hope possible without faith in a transcendent reality? Are the problems of human existence ones which are in principle within human competence to resolve or must the future inevitably involve men in the same fundamental human difficulties? Say that by the elaboration of medical techniques men could have great stretches of time, perhaps even endlessly extended, and the vigor to use it. Would that answer the problem of self-fulfillment? If being a man implies a sense of intellectual, aesthetic, and more particularly moral excellence, if it implies dissatisfaction with everything less than a fully integrated self in spirit and in action, man's problem is not time or technique but the distance between finite self and infinite aspiration. His problem lies in the quality of existence, and although man may modify it, he cannot change it. Even endless time could only bring man to despair, for with many years and undreamed-of help he still could not yet live life in the fullness he knows he ought to reach. Even without death to dramatize his limits, endless time itself could only bring him an endless sense of ultimate frustration.

If that is man's existential reality, then it would be absurd for him to face the future with an attitude so fundamentally positive as to be worthy of the term "hope." It is even more difficult to believe, except by some quixotic self-assertion against the universe, that he could in some secular fashion make hope the fundamental principle of his existence. As I see it, modern man's trust in the future must necessarily be self-contradictory. If we know nothing that can radically change the present, then the future can only mollify or alleviate our existential discontent. That sentiment, important and useful as it may be, hardly qualifies as hope. If we know that the years to come will be essentially as disquieting as now, though with some improvements and conveniences, then we should speak of our attitude toward them as expectation, anticipation, desire, or longing but something quite distinct from the old religious virtue, hope. And I believe a fresh look at modern man's continual concern with what is yet to be will show this, in fact, to be the case.

This, however, has led to a fundamental methodological problem, one which is insoluble, yet unavoidable. Out of the plethora of evidence available how does one know exactly what the secular mentality is? How can one be certain he is talking about modern man rather than his fantasies concerning him? Since secular man is considered scientifically oriented, one would think that empirical factors would be critical. Yet, as in the " death of God " dispute, the practice is to ignore such statistical data as exists, since it is assumed that most people are really behind the times. In talking of secular man, then, theologians are playing at spiritual sociology. I suppose the only way we shall know who is right is by applying one Biblical standard for prophecy and waiting to see whether things turn out as predicted. In the meantime the best thing such speculation can do is to provide a useful hermeneutic for understanding some of the movements in our society, though just which ones and how many one cannot say. I would suggest as one handy rule for understanding such analysis that we tend to find the significantly new in reaction to what we are tired of seeing. Again Hegel refuses to die. In the interpretation that follows I admit my amateur standing as a social diagnostician and confess that if there is anything I am overly acquainted with, it is Jewish secularity usurping Jewish religiosity.

I see modern man's concern for the future as quite spurious, a rationalization or an escape, but not a genuine hope. On one level I believe that is true because in substantial part we have had the experience of reaching a hoped-for future and finding it wanting. The American society has made a tremendous leap forward in the past two decades. Many, many people today — unfortunately not all — have had an entirely unexpected number of their fondest dreams fulfilled. The cars, the clothes, the homes, the vacations, the appliances, the recreation, are often far better than they ever could have imagined twenty years ago. Then they believed that if only they had this or that, they would be happy. Now they have been given much of what they had asked — and it has not solved anything. They do not want to go back to life as it was but they have learned, decisively I think, that having is not being. They may still want more and better things. That is only because the present might be better, not because they can any longer have genuine hope in the future. And the disappointment that has come to Communists with the achievement of communist states is a commonplace of the postmodern world.

That, it seems to me, explains why we are less oriented to the future than we are to the present. The most obvious economic fact of our times is not that people invest but that they live on credit, that they mortgage their future to pay for pleasures now. They do so because they do not trust in the future as much as their parents did. They cannot be certain they will ever get there, so everyone is on a pleasure spree, seeking to fill the now with the justification of existence. The squares experiment with restaurants and travel, the liberals with sex, and the radicals with drugs. Even the multimedia dance halls are no voyage into the future, only a nonpharmaceutical way of blotting out time by overloading the senses. I cannot see how we can ignore this massive redirection from the future to the present, nor do I see what else can explain it but our lack of faith in the future.

On a far more intellectual level, Albert Camus had seen this in the early 1940's. In his novel *The Plague* and elsewhere he characterized modern man as one who must learn to live without hope. If he is, by definition, a man who sacrifices all illusion to face reality, then the most dangerous illusion of all, the one he must therefore most thoroughly surrender, is hope. Camus knew that without some transcendent standard or reality the future could be no better than the past and he also knew transcendence was no longer accessible. Being as human as he was honest, he asked how man now could keep from despair, most radically suicide, and how he might come to exercise common decency toward others. He failed to validate ethics without transcendence, yet his quest remains a model for courageous secularity.

I have presented these three aspects of the modern experience not only to argue that it is not essentially future oriented but equally to call to mind its radical rejection of transcendence. If the theologian's apologetic strategy leads him to try explaining religious hope in secular terms, he must inevitably compromise the fundamental nature of the Biblical trust. The secular concern for the future and indeed its current escape into the present does afford religion an opportunity to speak of similar dissatisfactions which must similarly be met by faith. Still, at some point the apologetics must give way to a certain polemical thrust no matter in how friendly or open a way it is set forward. Surely no dialogue is worth entering into if one cannot stand one's own ground in full and equal dignity.

The strange fate of hope in modern Jewish history is worthy of special consideration in this regard. The old tripartite structure of Biblical personal, communal, eschatological hope held with some variety in the configuration throughout the Middle Ages. Then, with some individual cases such as Spinoza as exceptions, it was the concept of autonomy created by the Enlightenment, systematically elaborated by Kant and given special power by the secular state and modern science which required it to undergo major reconsideration. Validation now meant personal experience, rational, moral, or religious. Eschatology was the primary victim, for what could the individual personally know of what waited beyond historic times? The folk hope somehow managed to survive, though how personal evidence could mandate group existence was a problem that has continued to disturb Jewish theology down to the present more rigorously individualistic time. Hope for man still remained, since that was the dogmatic foundation of the concept of autonomy. If, then, the Jewish people helped individuals and even mankind, then one might hope that it would survive in history.

The holocaust under Hitler destroyed that liberal reconstruction and yet prevented a return to the traditional modes of belief. It was no longer possible to make the goodness of man the cornerstone of Jewish faith. Yet who could see God acting in this horror-filled history? That is not because it was traumatic. The Jewish people had been able to see God in disaster before. The prophetic interpretation of the Biblical catastrophes had long since set the standard that the Jews utilized to explain disasters as substantial as the destruction of the Second Temple, the defeat of Bar-Cochba, the expulsion from Spain, the rampage of Chmielnicki. None had caused a break with the Jewish tradition of hope, though it had often been reinterpreted. Now, however, the social suffering was too great to be seen as any sort of divine punishment or instruction. And the pain of endless individuals was too great to find explanation in the survival of the people or in such eschatological promises as might still be extended. If God did not act for individuals and Israel, then how could one hope that he would ever act again? How could one even trust that he was there?

It is characteristic of Judaism that if any new statement of atheism was to move the Jewish community after World War II, it had to come on the basis of what happened in history rather than because philosophers worried whether statements about God could have significant intellectual content. Jews for all their intellectuality do not seem so rationalistic as to consider that a compelling reason for saying that God is dead. And, in turn, they have been amazed that the major " death of God " thinkers have not discussed the unparalleled destruction of Jews under Hitler as a reason for disbelief in God. Yet that alone has agitated the Jewish community whenever it sought to speak of Jewish faith.

That social interpretation is, of course, subjective but, I think, quite widespread, which awakens the problem of how to read simple social evidence on an even more significant level. How does one know that this and not that event is revelatory? Why did the Hebrews say it was the exodus and Sinai and not the four-hundred-year slavery or the golden calf that taught them what was finally true and ultimately real? I do not know the answer to those questions. I only know that for me, and I believe for the Jewish people as a whole, the holocaust was shattering but not determinative. It was not the Sinai of our time. It burned us, tortured us, scarred us, and does so yet today. Nonetheless, its obscene brutality did not become our paradigm for future history. I have never been able to cease wondering, in the technical, Biblical sense, that after the holocaust there was no mass desertion of Judaism. If anything, there arose in the community as a whole a conscious desire to reclaim and reestablish Jewish existence. It was no more than that. Yet, considering what Jewishness had just entailed, that spontaneous, inner reassertion was uncanny. It testified to that which is more than man's wisdom and courage, which yet sustains and carries him through the terrors of personal and social history. I find it also important, though of lesser significance, that today, despite substantial publicity to a community generally recognized as highly secularized, the Jewish " death of God " movement has had very little acceptance. I attribute this to the social fact that whereas hearing of religious atheists sounds new and radical to others, to Jews it is somehow very old-fashioned. Atheism is where we all were in the thirties and the forties in the days when we still thought university rationalism would redeem the world. That is what those of us who still care about Judaism seriously turned from, so to revive it now for a new Judaism seems strangely behind the times. What is more important, the very phenomenon it should explain it instead destroys. To say that there is no God means that everything is permitted. Now the holocaust, because it is explained, is neutralized. It does not even have a negative power. By what right are we disgusted, nauseated, overwhelmed, outraged, at what took place to the innocent if it was only an honest reflection of reality and not an intolerable violation of a standard of right inherent in the universe itself? The new atheism would rob Jews of their moral indignation, and it is just that which the Jewish community knows better than to surrender. Some decades back it could be tolerant of an atheism that left ethics standing. Today secular ethics is a vanishing myth and atheism means nihilism. That is to lose the very moral ground from which the protest against God was launched.

Postholocaust Jewish theology found itself in a period where only a negative methodology might be intellectually bearable, though hardly emotionally effective. Any effort to explain the holocaust would by that very fact betray the event and the reactions to it. So nothing could be said. Yet unbelief was equally impossible because of the moral affirmation inherent in the very protest. Jews could not speak but many also could not not believe. They could only have a theology of non-non-belief. That was not much but it was more than nothing. Considering what Jews had been through, considering that some Jews standing before us had been through it and refused not to believe, that would have been enough to be the realistic content of Jewish hope in history.

Now, once again, historic events have shaken Jews to their foundations. To speak of Jewish hope today means discussing the June 1967 Arab-Israeli war and within the Biblical frame of reference. Hope for the individual Jew was until recent times intimately linked with the fate of his people, and what happened to the Jewish people in history affected the individual Jew's sense of personal hope insofar as it was founded on Jewish faith. That personal-communal relationship stems from Israel's Covenant with God. The individual Jew shares God's Covenant as one of the people of Israel, and that means that he is by divine act tied to all Jews, everywhere in the world, especially those who live in the Land of Israel, and his destiny is necessarily linked with theirs. That ethnic closeness in a religious faith may be more than what one normally expects in a church, but God called the children of Israel to him as a folk and not as a church. That social structure has over the ages been found fully appropriate to its purpose of endurance through history.

Jewish hope, moreover, is linked to what God does in historic time. If the Jews find themselves in a house of bondage, they await God's saving action in the here and now. That was the trauma of the holocaust. If one is to speak of Jewish hope, one must speak of the fate of Jews, and that means, among other communities, particularly the State of Israel. That sounds like politics to many Christians and hence strangely unreligious. But Christian categories will not do here. The destiny of the Household of Israel is a theopolitical matter now as it was in Biblical times. Neither man's institutions for channeling governmental power nor God's concern with what this people must yet do in history can be eliminated when discussing the Jews and their Judaism.

That Monday afternoon when the war began and no news of what was taking place came through, there was black anxiety throughout the Jewish world. The question was not military, who would win. It was theological. Would God abandon the people of Israel again and allow the citizens of the State of Israel to be slaughtered by Arab armies? For weeks Jews had heard of radio Cairo's threats to exterminate the Jews of the State of Israel and had watched on television as the mobs there and in other Arab capitals were whipped into a frenzied hatred of the Israelis. The danger was real and not exaggerated. If the Arab armies drove back the Israelis, there would be an incredible massacre against which the Western governments would not intercede in time. And God had already shown once this century that he could withdraw from history sufficiently to allow his people to be slaughtered. Could Judaism survive another holocaust? It was not, then, only the Israeli armies who were on trial that day but, in very earnest, God himself.

Then came the victory, clean, sharp, and decisive; gained by intelligence and skill backed by moral will and determination; unsullied by brutality, vengefulness, atrocity, or vindictiveness. We sophisticates thought we knew historical reality and therefore had discounted much of the Bible. Now before our very eyes history turned Biblical once again. Of course it was relief, elation, a victory at last and a great one. That only begins the explanation, for the truth is that to their own surprise many Jews recognized the presence of a transcendent reality operating in history that they had almost come to believe could no longer make itself felt there. They knew all the technical reasons for the Israeli success but they also knew these did not explain what had taken place. Without soldiers and generals, without equipment and training, nothing could have happened. What happened, however, was more than what they alone could do, and so Jews naturally and necessarily gave thanks to Him who works wonders and delivers his people from Egypt. Jews saw him once again as he who remembers his Covenant. I am not saying that the Israeli victory proves to Jews that there is a God. I am saying that what happened in June spoke to most Jews in a way that, for example, the Sinai campaign of 1956 did not. For a moment the tight naturalistic structure through which secularized men see everything cracked open and we saw him. So one cannot speak of Jewish hope today as we would have done after the holocaust but before the war.

The reader will have noticed that I have not spoken of what happened to them, there in the State of Israel, but of what happened to us, the Jews. This was, of course, the Israelis' politics, their war, and their immediate suffering. Although American Jews are not bound to them politically, they were by virtue of being one people under God intimately involved in their crisis. How could Jews who have been through this holocaust and postholocaust era together now stand divided in trial or in triumph? Perhaps neither of us knew how closely we felt tied to them until the moment of crisis arrived. It is certain that neither of us realized how deeply we were still rooted in Jewish tradition until we all stood once again, so unexpectedly, before the Western Wall of the Temple in Old Jerusalem. Irony of ironies, it is that archaic religious symbol which more than anything else explains to agnostics and to liberals, to secularists and to the nonobservant, who the people of Israel is.

So in one incredible week Jews reclaimed two strands of their old Jewish hope. They saw God save the people of Israel and recognized personally how their individual being was tied to the Covenant folk. And now many could feel free to speak of what had sounded so hollow in the postholocaust days, that they have from time to time felt his help and presence in their own lives. In the face of the people's disaster, schooled in secular disbelief, how could they say God still works in human lives and have hope in him? Now what they have seen broadcast before the entire world makes it possible to say in all humility, he has helped individuals too. The experience of the community is once again linked with that of the individual and the old pattern of Covenant hope on these two levels has reasserted itself.

What has been regained is not a soothing, easy hope. It encompasses of necessity the reality of pain, even of incredible suffering. It does not relish such experiences nor find them a virtue to be cherished. The suffering of the servant has been foisted on Jews. The crucifixion is not a model for them. Gladly would they await the Messiah with the normal tests of endurance. Yet in the midst of whatever bondage history may now bring, Jews can once again hope in God's action on their behalf. He did so for the fathers. He did so in this time. They trust he will do so again for their children and their children's children as he promised. His Covenant with Israel remains intact.

Jewish theologians do not understand how to explain in technically coherent terms this strange history of service, of suffering, and of continued hope. What has recently been seen gives no intellectual clarity about the continuing problems of individual Jews and Jewish communities, of persons and peoples of every faith and none. Nothing can still be said about the holocaust. History is grimmer than ever imagined and human existence far more difficult than previously believed. Still, amid that realism, there is a Jew's sense of hope. God may try Israel, even turn away from it, but he does not entirely abandon or forget it. Neither individual existence nor social destiny escapes his saving power. In such a world as ours that is a lot to know. It is the only kind of hope that has a chance to be the answer to despair.

Knowing that much, must not even secularized Jews follow the organic development of Biblical Judaism and move on from personal and social hope to a full-throated eschatological belief? Such a belief surely is incompatible with secularity, but now that the secular has been transcended in historic reality the next step is to reassert in contemporary accents the coming of his Kingdom which will transform and redeem history. That is more than can be easily said at present. Indeed, already the cynics and the sophisticated are eager to analyze away the religious reality of what was so freshly gained. I trust that despite their numbers and their stature they will not succeed but rather that the promise of the unknown prophet of the exile will be fulfilled:

> Why sayest thou, O Jacob,
> And speakest, O Israel:
> " My way is hid from the LORD,

And my right is passed over from my God "?
Hast thou not known? hast thou not heard
That the everlasting God, the LORD,
The Creator of the ends of the earth,
Fainteth not, neither is weary?
His discernment is past searching out.
He giveth power to the faint:
And to him that hath no might He increaseth strength.
Even the youths shall faint and be weary,
And the young men shall utterly fall;
But they that wait for the LORD shall renew their strength;*
They shall mount up with wings as eagles;
They shall run, and not be weary;
They shall walk, and not faint.

(Isa. 40:27-31.)

---

* Note that those who hope in God do not always have the strength they need to meet history. They may be weary of running and faint from walking. What they receive from the Lord is not exemption from history but the assurance of strength, his strength infusing theirs.

PART
II

THE PEOPLE COVENANTED TO HIM

Chapter

4

CELEBRATING THE REVELATION
AT SINAI

The problem of the continuing observance of Shavuot, the Feast of Weeks, is both the Biblical story itself and the legal discipline that claims to derive from it. The question is hardly whether the mountain was on fire, a horn sounded, or the people " saw " thunder.[1] The Bible reports and the holiday service celebrates God's giving words of instruction to his people. Some he himself said for all the people to hear; the rest he spoke to Moses to say to them. The rabbinic tradition authorized itself by saying that God also gave Moses either in principle or in detail the teaching which was to be handed down orally but authoritatively from generation to generation by the teachers of the law. Shavuot celebrates God's giving of the words of the Torah, both written and oral, and I cannot believe that. With all the love and respect I have for the Jewish tradition and its wisdom, which regularly far surpasses my own, I cannot believe that God reveals himself in words. My reasons do not fully explain the reality of my faith as I try to live it, but two critical considerations affect me. Even in the moments of which I can say I have been closest and most intimate with God, I have not found him speaking words — though that may only prove what I well know, that I am no prophet. When I consider the words that others have heard which they said were God's own (though of course put in human terms), it seems far more consistent with everything else I at this point know of man's history and God's nature that these are men's own words in response to God, not his dictation.

In my opinion, the most characteristic theological assertion of liberal Judaism is that such knowledge as men have of God is subjective, a human response to him, rather than objective human reception of his formulations.[2] It is this personal grounding of revelation which makes for the fundamental liberalism of modern Judaism, that is, its effort to maximize religious freedom of choice and its trust in the responsible individual. Theoreticians may disagree to what extent God is actively involved in the process of man's coming to know Him, arguing in humanistic versions that religious knowledge is really self-knowledge for which "revelation" is hardly an appropriate term. Because I believe God still has an active role in such human experience, I still want to speak of revelation, though I do not believe in verbal revelation. Regardless of the term used and its special nuances, the liberal Jewish thinkers, almost without exception, are united in their insistence on the subjectivity of man's knowledge of God.

If Shavuot is traditionally the great Jewish commemoration of God's objective revelation, how can those who affirm its subjectivity celebrate Shavuot?

It will help to begin with some phenomenological observations, with the reality of the given situation. It has the advantage of preventing the continuing regress to basic assumptions which soon undercuts every attempt to analyze a complex, synthesizing theological symbol such as Sinai. To be sure, the phenomenological basis chosen will necessarily seem arbitrary to some and may therefore appear to provide a skewed or perverted sample of experience to be analyzed. Such subjectivity is not to be avoided, and with that recognition the following observations are the foundation for this discussion: (1) Liberal Jews celebrate the Festival of Shavuot essentially in a communal, liturgical manner, and though its observance does not resolve all their questions concerning the Festival, they know it is expressive of their relation to God. (2) They observe Shavuot in their way as a continuation of a traditional observance of the Jewish people. They did not originate this day; neither have they rejected it as they did certain other Jewish practices. (3) At the same time, it is a Reform innovation in the commemoration, the confirmation ceremony, which makes the day most meaningful.

Analysis of so rich a human experience should be undertaken with a certain humility. The past century and a half of liberal expositions of the meaning of Jewish practice should have demonstrated that observances remain more meaningful than analyses of them can disclose. Liturgy and ritual are a creative language of their own and not merely a primitive substitute for the philosopher or social scientist or theologian's self-consciousness. The validation of the observance comes in the practice itself, not in its abstract discussion. Yet the elucidation of the meanings implicit in religious activity has an important place in religion: men are morally obligated to know what they can and thus increase the responsibility of their decisions. Such knowledge may shape even if it does not determine a man's deeds as he seeks to live his faith. This discussion, then, does not seek to exhaust the meanings of Shavuot or to validate it but in accordance with this heuristic understanding of the theology of ritual, to make plain some of the meaning that seems to continue to move Jews.

It will also save some needless argument to clarify what Jews are not required to celebrate on Shavuot day, namely, the legendary associations of the revelation at Sinai. Here the tradition was already quite clear. The halachic regimen for the observance of Shavuot does not obligate the Jew to affirm the historicity of every rabbinic hyperbole on the giving of the Torah, e.g., that the whole world was silent or that the Decalogue was heard in seventy different languages around the world when God spoke.[3] The authority of the halachah does not extend to such details despite the occasional efforts of zealots to turn *aggada* into dogma. Such midrashic allusions occur only in the liturgical poetry and not even in all of it, for these hymns are far more concerned to stress the greatness of the Ten Commandments and the Torah than the legends that surround the day.[4] Since such legendary material as does occur is limited to this poetic context, it should be clear that it need not be taken literally. Liberal Jews, whose passion for the chronological is well developed, should have little difficulty distinguishing rabbinic elaboration from Biblical account.

Yet the fundamental difficulties involved in the reconciliation required here have in no way been eased. Before undertaking such an enterprise it will also help to set forth the historical-intellectual frame in which it is offered. One advantage of the many varieties of liberal Jewish thought over the past century and a half is that they have explored a number of available alternatives. By exposing the consequences implicit in various theological perspectives, they have made it easier for succeeding thinkers to know which assumptions deny or require the sort of Jewish religious existence that they somehow know to be true for them. This is particularly true in that most perplexing of all liberal Jewish theological problems: What does God still require Jews to do? A typology of the answers given thus far would find them clustering around two poles. The one set seeks to derive practice largely from a conception of God. The other speaks more of the peculiar practice of the people of Israel.

The earlier views see religious practice as a celebration and rehearsal of the unity of God — most often as eternal ethical principles derived from the acknowledgment of his overarching oneness. Shavuot thus celebrates the supreme ethical discovery and commitment of the Jewish people. True monotheism (the first three commandments) is the necessary foundation for all true morality (the last six commandments). The difficulty with all such theories is the logical inconsistency of seeking to justify particular actions by universal values. They can never satisfactorily explain why, now that the universal values are known in a truly universal way, anyone need bother to practice them in a highly particular fashion, e.g., on the sixth of Sivan, which falls on a Friday (as in 5729, 1969). The answers attempted have never been convincing. Some have argued that the Jewish idea of God was unique, or that Jewish ethics were unique, or that Jewish ethical monotheism was unique and required the Jewish people to make it manifest in history.[5] Yet if God and ethics are truly universal, they cannot be especially Jewish, except by accident of discovery. Hegel, the unwitting source of the concept that most connects universal ideas with a particular people (and its celebrations), already provides its refutation. Now that the ideas have risen to the state of full, self-conscious, philosophic reflection, their religious elaboration, less pure and less universal, is superseded effectively. Since one knows, one need not celebrate. Pragmatic arguments (the help religious observances give in opening man to ethical monotheism or keeping him faithful to it) will not help much. Try justifying the Fourth Commandment this way! The Sabbath is not directly an ethical activity, and surely one could get more direct aid for one's ethical aspirations in contemporary society by Sunday rather than by Saturday observance, and by recreation and education rather than by liturgy and sanctification, though all non-Orthodoxy has steadfastly called for the primacy of the latter. The argument is even weaker with a Shavuot that falls on a Friday. The theological reasoning the average Jew derives from this universalist, God-centered view is impeccable; if he believes in the one God and does the right thing, isn't he really a good Jew though he doesn't come to temple or observe Shavuot? The liberals taught him well, unfortunately, and must bear intellectual responsibility for his minimal observance.

The counterargument seeks to emphasize the ethnic element in Jewish existence and, by authorizing the particular group, to motivate the Jewish form of observing. This position is even less satisfactory to the American Jew whose sociological strivings to be an equal reinforce his intellectual insistence on validation in terms of universals or autonomy. The ethnicists are led either into chauvinism, social determinism, or social utilitarianism. So one hears that Jews have a racial talent for religion, or that one is requried by the laws of sociology to express one's religion through one's people, or that it is best for one's mental health not to reject one's group; or that it will be a way to enrich one's cultural existence by amplifying it with these old folk functions.[6] An individual might well derive some personal satisfactions from joining his people's folk festivals, though I doubt that one would get very far with a Friday Shavuot by such reasoning. Moreover, why unless God is somehow real and present to this people, should they make his formal worship the focus of their late-spring festivities? After all, the holiday traditionally celebrates his doing more than the Jewish people's being, and it gives them little positive to do other than to pray to God and to rehearse his goodness toward them.

Contrasting these ideas vis-à-vis Jewish practice (a good Jewish way of pursuing this unaccustomed intellectual enterprise), one may learn that any theology of Jewish observance which does not include both a real and present God and some sort of special relationship between him and the people of Israel will not result in any meaningful continuation of traditional practices. If there is no God, Jews can at best celebrate themselves or be that antiquarian-minded remnant of humanity which still takes time out (on a Friday morning?) to remember one interesting day in an Arabian peninsula (though rationally they should free themselves of this cultural laggardness and give over their limited celebration time to more directly significant events in man's self-understanding, i.e., Freud's discovery of the unconscious). At the same time, if Israel does not have some special link with God, then Jews might just as well celebrate their individual belief all by themselves. Private celebration will be not only more convenient but less fraught with the risks of boredom and personal irritation which are the steady threat of public worship. Because many are not willing to face up to what they believe about God, many a Shavuot celebration quietly substitutes the aesthetic experience for the liturgical, the impressive dramatic reading for the communal reliving of what God did at Sinai. And because others — though far fewer, I think, than once was true — are not clear about the corporate nature of the Jew's relation to God, such liturgies as are created for the confirmands sound, except for a few Hebrew sentences and modes, more like public high school baccalaureate exercises than the people of Israel renewing its Covenant and its task. Thus a Jewish theology that will be adequate to the religious realities of the continuing observance of Shavuot must somehow know a real

God and a significantly unique bond between him and the congregation of Israel. And that experience/knowledge is the framework within which I seek to clarify what I solemnize at Shavuot.

Though I cannot commemorate the giving of the Torah in the objective sense that traditional Judaism understood it, I celebrate the establishment and the continual reestablishment of the relationship between God and Israel. I rejoice in *kiyum brit*, the inauguration of the full Covenant with the Israelite people rather than *matan torah*, the giving of the body of law and instruction by which it was to be lived. The one is basic to the other. I accept the fundamental God-Israel relationship. So do those who go beyond it to accept also its verbal quality and accompanying rabbinic interpretation. As one who affirms that Covenant as the foundation of his existence, I too acknowledge that I stand under the law. Only for me the law is not identical with the written or the oral law of tradition. Rather, it is that living discipline which flows from the consciousness of standing in direct personal relationship with God, not merely as a private self, but as one of the community with whom he has covenanted. Although I cannot agree that the pact between God and Israel established at Sinai was fixed then in immutable, contractual terms (together with the principles of their extension and elaboration over the generations), I know that a relationship is meaningful only insofar as it results in action, that Covenant without responsibility, faith without deed, is meaningless. My sense of obligation under the Covenant is more dynamic and less institutional than the traditional, but it too rests on what happened at Sinai and was recapitulated in later generations, as today on Shavuot. So establishing the relationship is my equivalent to " the giving of the law."

This understanding clarifies, it seems to me, the nature of my observance.

I celebrate the traditional holiday, on the traditional date, with liturgical forms that are substantially traditional. The Covenant did not begin with me. I came into it when I was born; it was, so to speak, there waiting for me. It belongs to history. If it depended on me and my abilities to initiate such a covenant from the human side, I do not think there would be a covenant. I know I am not what Father Abraham was; but because he was, I can try to emulate him.

The Covenant is not carried through history or renewed by me alone. It did not remain the possession of one family for long. Indeed, the first man of the Covenant was promised that he would become a father of nations, a mighty people. He had to be in order to enter and survive and transform human history. Sinai is the culmination of the Covenant with Abraham, the inception of its full form, not a Covenant with Moses, but one with all the Household of Israel. So I, who affirm that relationship, am not free to choose a private date or time to celebrate the establishment of my people's relationship with God. I celebrate it on our day, in their midst, and, essentially by liturgy, for our relationship is with Him, the real and present God, the living God. We rejoice not simply with one another, but with him, for what we celebrate is that we know him and continue to serve him, and that of all human communities ours has been permitted to have had this intimate and continuing experience of him.

The traditional Jew, looking at my observance, will find many of its features strange. He will be particularly perplexed that I interpret *brit* in personal rather than in legal terms.[7] But he should be able to recognize (and that is increasingly my experience) that what unites him and me is greater than what separates us. We stand as part of the same Jewish people united in the same basic relationship wtih the same God. (Because one does not need to define someone to have an authentic relationship with him, the issues of the identity of our concepts of God is as irrelevant to this dimension of the discussion as to the traditional *aggada*.) We both believe that this Covenant relationship authorizes and requires communal and individual action. We differ only — though it is a great Jewish "only" — on what constitutes that required action, its substance, hierarchy, and religious weight.

Because the partners of the relationship have remained substantially the same over the centuries, though the terms used to describe them have differed, the sort of action that derives from the relationship will remain recognizably continuous with what went before. However, new social circumstances and intellectual insights may make it possible to enrich and enhance, as they may require Jews to modify or to reject, the old patterns of living the Covenant. The confirmation ceremony is an excellent example because its proper practice is already its justification.

The tradition knows no such group rite: [8] for girls as well as for boys; at the conclusion of a prescribed course of study; at an age well past thirteen; as part of the Shavuot liturgy; climaxed by an act of dedication on the children's part. Reform Jews may have dropped the celebration of the second day, the *musaf*, the additional festival liturgy, and the customary *piyyutim*, the religious poetry. They may have modified the *birchat hashashar*, the opening prayers, and condensed the *shacharit*, the regular morning service. None of these touches the heart of the relationship to God nor deprives the congregation of the central means of sanctifying the day. To the contrary, the reality of that Covenant relationship comes alive for moderns precisely because its ancient feel is conveyed in the modern mode by an air of serious attention, harmonic music, understandable prayers, family seating — and, most of all, by the confirmation ceremony itself.

What is being done with these young people? They cannot now be inducted into the congregation of Israel and its millennial responsibilities since they have been part of it from birth. That was imposed upon them, a necessity, so to speak, of being born to just this family. Now, however, they may turn destiny into personal choice. At confirmation they are welcomed to conscious, individual affirmation of God's Covenant with Israel. That is why they had to study before they ascended the pulpit; they had to know what history had bequeathed to them so that they could know what burdens they must carry. That is why they had to be of a more mature age than thirteen, so that their understanding could be fuller and their affirmation more responsible. (Why not at the end of high school, an even more mature and critical time?) So girls as well as boys are included, for the Covenant relationship is as real with women as it is with men. So, too, the ceremony involves a group of young people, in the presence of a great and numerous congregation, for the Covenant is no private matter but one which binds private souls to the people of Israel's pact. That is why it takes place on Shavuot day, for that is the day when the Israelite folk itself had to decide whether to accept God's Covenant relationship. Now each year the Sinai day rolls round and the faithfulness of Israel to that ancient pledge is once more tested (as in so many other ways) and — how surprisingly for this stiff-necked folk — once again renewed. The confirmation children join all the Children of Israel in their rededication, only they do so publicly, formally, in a way that therefore marks a turning point in their Jewish development. They may soon not care, or rebel, or quietly turn to things that are more fun. It is their privilege, to use their freedom for good or ill. Yet the people of Israel did its duty by them and by their God in helping them to know that precious, sacred history and by inviting them to personal appropriation of that untiring messianic task.

That is why the congregation is so moved by the ceremony. Of course, it is sentiment mixed with guilt, the consciousness of aging fused with the illusions associated with the children. Yet these are not base emotions, unworthy of bearing God's truth or sensitizing men to his presence. The worshipers may not have been the Jews they ought to have been, the Jews their parents or grandparents or rabbis wished them to be. They may have failed the children often as they sought to guide them, and they hide from rather than acknowledge what they have repaid God for his benefits. But on Shavuot day, in the sanctuary, seeing the children on his altar, this Sinai, hearing them affirm and avow and depose and declare, they know they have not been altogether faithless. By bringing them to confirmation, they have confirmed their loyalty, and confirming them, the adults are confirmed as well. That is true not only for the parents of the confirmands but for every Jew who identifies himself with the Jewish community and shares in its mutual responsibility for the education of all Jewish children. The confirmands are the Jews' children, the next necessary step in the people's purposeful history, the hope that the Covenant effort will continue yet farther into history, working and waiting for the Kingdom of God.

Traditional Judaism knew no such ceremony as confirmation, but if Shavuot day celebrates the establishment of God's Covenant with Israel, what act could be more relevant? Indeed, it illuminates and upholds the rest, for at least Jews still love their children, though they find it difficult to understand, much less practice, the love of God. (That is why some Shavuot services are exercises in the manipulation of congregational emotions rather than an openness to confrontation with the covenanting God.)

There remains one last question, the most crucial of all. Its several forms are one: Did God really make a Covenant with Israel? Is it true that God has a special relationship with Israel? How do you know? How can you believe this? " Really . . . true . . . know . . . believe . . . how," these are the words that chart the regress of every theological assertion back to ontology, epistemology, and beyond, to those fundamental assertions which turn the chaos of the fully open mind into the creation called premises or assumptions. To answer requires a radical return to the first questions of theological methodology and thence a gradual working out of these initial principles until they reach Sinai and thus Shavuot. That is, no less, the demand for a systematic Jewish theology. Yet the question cannot altogether be set aside here, for if nothing really happened at Sinai, if nothing could have happened at Sinai, then for all its intellectual utility, the Covenant theory is meaningless.

Without seeking to duplicate in Jewish circles the debate that Rudolf Bultmann's radical rejection of historicity continues to evoke among Protestants, this much may be said: what " really " happened at Sinai lies outside the sphere of the modern academic discipline known as history.[9] The historian, as historian, can tell us something about the records and traditions of the Sinaitic Covenant. He will want to have his say in the continuing argument over the likely date of the exodus and how many of the Hebrew tribes were involved in the Egyptian experience. He may even be able to contribute something about how the events described as taking place at Sinai compare with similar events in the history of other peoples. What he cannot suggest, as long as he sticks strictly to historic evidence, is whether God and Israel did in fact make such a Covenant. This question involves fundamental metaphysical questions to which his historical evidence is irrelevant: Is there a God? Does he act? Does he make covenants? Normally, historians are reticent about their implicit metaphysics, admitting that what they offer is an imaginative reconstruction of the past which is as valid as their premises about what "really" powers and shapes history. The latter, being a metaphysical matter, they generally do not argue but accept as a matter of modern methodology or good academic discipline. What is vital to this discussion is that good modern methodology involves leaving God out as an active factor in history. It is one thing to state this as a methodological procedure. It is quite another to claim it as a statement of reality. A modern historian cannot say much about what happened at Sinai because his very methodology prevents him from knowing a God who acts in history, but because he cannot detect this reality with his specialized instruments does not yet mean that what the texts say took place did not take place.[10]

The same is true of the contributions of the psychologist, the anthropologist, and other social scientists. They may disclose much about religious behavior; what they cannot assess is whether religion is true. Their very methodology (since it is rigidly empirical) prevents them from knowing God and hence they are incompetent to deal with the most vital of all religious questions. They do not know what is real because they cannot know it until they forsake scientific method for metaphysics.

Philosophy then stands between me and the Shavuot services. In recent Jewish history, philosophy was less a menace than a friend.[11] Neo-Kantian ethicism and post-Hegelian historicism seemed ideal means of expressing ancient Jewish themes in modern tones. They could do this because each in its own way could show what then seemed rational access to metaphysical reality. Kant knew no metaphysics of the natural order, but he clearly asserted the validity of the noumenal order reached via ethics. Hegel saw the one absolute spirit making itself manifest in the zigzag of historic development. Religion therefore could be substantiated by philosophy and yet remain reasonably true to its own personal and historic genius.

Contemporary philosophy is nowhere nearly so hospitable to religion. If anything, its antimetaphysical compulsions make it downright hostile. Linguistic analysis is generally as atheistic as its parent, logical positivism. Phenomenology and existentialism are resolute in their rejection of the claims that there is a God. Such occasional metaphysical assertion as is still heard labors mightily to bring forth some sense of ultimate reality, but does so under the handicap that most modern philosophers consider that task, much less their results, well outside the limits of the acceptable use of the term " rational."

These metaphysical issues are not to be dismissed. They are not trivial. If what religion is speaking about is to be made meaningful, it must somehow come to terms with modern philosophic idiom, even if that means to fight, refine, or even break modern philosophy's constricted sense of what can be real. Although the average man or the educated man who comes to the service is unaware of this technical philosophical discussion, he nonetheless reflects it in the covert metaphysics upon which, quite unwittingly, he builds his life. Religion cannot altogether ignore the issues posed by contemporary philosophy even though they seem in our day, as against what they were in another generation of liberal Judaism, to reject the possibility of meaningful religion.

Now, however, as I begin to ponder these questions for the hundredth time, I realize that the fifth of Sivan is drawing to a close. Shavuot is upon me with its claim for observance. I will not have time to resolve these metaphysical problems before the holiday is here. If I insist on doing so I shall almost certainly never observe the Festival this year. My insistence on clarifying all the premises of religion before I move on to religious practice will, in effect, be the equivalent of denying belief in God and the Covenant he entered into with Israel at Sinai.

To affirm the Covenant, however, need not mean one has resolved all the metaphysical issues inherent in that belief. I have
not. The question of my response to the coming of the sixth of
Sivan hinges rather on whether, despite all my doubts and difficulties, I still manage to believe enough that I can accept the ad-
vent of the Festival; whether my sense of what is finally real in
the universe is such that I can still go to meet my God as one of
his covenanted people.

I do not go to Shavuot services out of dogmatic security, but
despite my unanswered questions and unresolved conflicts, out of
a knowledge of what has happened to me there before, and not
just on this festival but day by day as I have tried to live under
the Covenant. And I am grateful to have discovered that, though
some of my problems with Judaism deepen as the years go by,
the question of whether I possess sufficient affirmation to attend
to this observance, as to many others, has grown less difficult to
answer positively.

If I am to lead the service, this knowledge that the service justifies itself imposes special responsibilities upon me. It cannot today
be only a fulfillment of the previously existing Jewish piety; it
must be an experience in Jewish rediscovery and reaffirmation. It
cannot simply count on what the modern, secularized congregation brings with it; it must reach out to them so that they know
as they can in so few other ways truly know, that God and Israel
still stand bound in Covenant.

The leader must manage the service. But if his mind is on the
organist's cues, the undependable microphone, the inattentive ush-
ers, or the nervous confirmation class, he will never bring to bear
the personal *kavvannah*, the devotion, which will mold sound and
music, silence and movement, reading and response, into living
liturgy. No wonder Roman Catholic tradition prescribes a master
of ceremonies to stand beside the officiant and guide him through
the intricate order of the special mass so that he may concentrate
on the meaning of what he is doing rather than on keeping order!
The Jewish prayer leader cannot shirk his responsibility in trans-
forming an audience into a congregation, but only as he transcends

techniques and leads the praying will the congregation come jointly to face its God.

That too is why the service itself is no time for metaphysical reflection. Precise meanings and integrated intellectual structures will have to wait for later. Now is the time to say what can be said and see what happens. Of course, one phrase or another may stick in the throat or be rejected by the mind as an honest expression of the whole self. Sometimes a whole paragraph may seem unsayable — though I am inclined to believe that many people so enjoy the posture of complaining about the prayer book that they cannot pray what, if they stopped posing, they could pray. Even to interrupt the service with many comments about the prayers, their meaning or origin, is to objectify the mood and shatter the developmental integrity of the service, thereby defeating the hope of making the festival worship a personal experience of Israel's communal Covenant reality. Thinking is no less present to the person for being subordinated now to what the whole man finds himself in this congregation at this moment able to say.

Yet any possibility of accomplishing this small liturgical miracle depends on what happens in the prayer leader himself. Jewish worshipers may once have been far more self-sufficient. Today modern calls for decorum have made them highly dependent on the man who stands before them. Most of the time his person will establish the context of what may happen at the service. He cannot not know this. In part, what attracted him to the rabbinate or cantorate was that he might be the focus of this community. Now he will read or sing or bless or speak and they will attend to him — and there will be many, many watching, listening, in a special mood of attention. If he does not gratify himself on this occasion, he will surely not be able to give to it the fullness of self on which all else hinges. But if he does so only to gratify himself, he has required his people to covenant with him rather than with God. True, he cannot deny his ego and its needs. Yet he can and must find a way in this vortex of institutional, intellectual, and emotional demands to be a transparent witness to the reality of the Covenant which binds this people to its God. Standing beyond drive and mind and ego, he must serve God with a whole heart.

Such accomplishment is not credible. The Household of Israel is too impious, the synagogue too bourgeois, the rabbi too human, God too distant. That is all true — and yet it happens. It has happened in the past — were the vessels of God's covenanting inhumanly saintly in Biblical times? And it has happened to many Jews on and off who found themselves one Sabbath, one holy day, one weekday, entering the service just people and becoming in it once again the people of his Covenant.

I cannot know whether it will happen once again this sixth of Sivan. I cannot tell what difference it will make if nothing special happens. Nevertheless, I know that if without tears or tongues or thrills or sparks something does happen, I shall probably recognize it as something old and familiar. It will not be altogether new and strange. When the service comes alive, Jews are not converted, only returned, restored, renewed. They discover what was ever theirs. They gain what they always had.

NOTES: *Chapter 4*

1. Ex. 20:18. Note the characteristic difference of interpretation between Ishmael and Akiba in *Mechilta Bachodesh* (Lauterbach ed., The Jewish Publication Society of America, 1933), Ch. 9, lines 1–5.

2. Gunther Plaut's insistence on the reality of revelation to the early Reformers is not in any way a contradiction of what is being asserted here, as the excerpts he gives demonstrate (*The Rise of Reform Judaism* [World Union for Progressive Judaism, 1963], p. 125).

3. For a typical collection, see Louis Ginzberg, *The Legends of the Jews* (The Jewish Publication Society of America, 1913), Vol. 3, pp. 90 ff., and Vol. 6, p. 35, n. 198.

4. A complete list with brief description is given by Abraham Idelsohn, *Jewish Liturgy* (Henry Holt & Company, Inc., 1932), in Appendix C. See especially pp. 336–337. It is noteworthy that the Hertz and Birnbaum prayer books for the entire year and the

Rabbinical Council of America prayer book for Sabbath and Festivals consider only the *Akdamut* of sufficient importance to warrant inclusion in their volumes. It contains no legendary material.

5. The Pittsburgh Platform in its very first article asserts the superiority of Israel's God-idea and then goes on in Articles 3 and 4 to set up universal ethics as the criterion of religious practice. David Philipson, *The Reform Movement in Judaism* (The Macmillan Company, 1907), p. 491. Despite Ahad Ha'am's championing of the idea of a unique Jewish ethical understanding and the many Reform Jewish Neo-Kantians who have placed great stress on Jewish ethics, no work since that of Moritz Lazarus has appeared which would seek to define those ethics or to indicate their unique approach. For the latter view, see Leo Baeck, *The Essence of Judaism* (1st English tr., The Macmillan Company, 1936), pp. 281 ff., and the entire first book of *This People Israel* (Holt, Rinehart & Winston, Inc., 1964).

6. So Geiger and Kohler are racialists, though they used the term far more loosely than we do. *Jewish Theology* (Riverdale Press, 1943), pp. 325 ff. See the justified attacks by Mordecai M. Kaplan in *Judaism as a Civilization* (Toronto: The Macmillan Company, 1934), p. 119, and his return to the attack over two decades later, as if the idea were still widespread, in *The Greater Judaism in the Making* (Reconstructionist Press, 1960), pp. 291 ff. Kaplan's own position is a mixture of the last two views, that one cannot fight social necessity and that one can benefit by accepting it. See *Judaism as a Civilization*, pp. 48, 184, 261.

7. In Biblical usage it often carries the connotation of specified law rather than relationship, e.g., Ps. 25:10 as contrasted with Ps. 44:17.

8. Although in 1831 a prominent Orthodox rabbi had already begun conducting regular confirmation ceremonies for classes of boys and girls (art. " Confirmation," *The Jewish Encyclopedia*, Vol. IV, pp. 219 f.).

9. For a survey of the question, see James M. Robinson, *A New Quest of the Historical Jesus* (SCM Press, Ltd., 1959), particularly pp. 1–25. For a Jewish reaction, see Lou Silberman, " The

New Quest for the Historical Jesus," *Judaism*, Vol. 11, No. 3 (Summer, 1962).

10. The many problems relative to the creation of a philosophy of history can only be noted here. For a good, brief summary of the range of issues from the standpoint of philosophy of religion, see John A. Hutchison, *Faith, Reason, and Existence* (Oxford University Press, 1956), pp. 167 ff. A review of the problem, which sketches the history of philosophy and theology of history from the earliest time to the present, is Alan Richardson, *History, Sacred and Profane* (The Westminster Press, 1964).

11. This theme is discussed in greater detail in my *Layman's Introduction to Religious Existentialism* (The Westminster Press, 1965), pp. 69 ff.

Chapter

5

WHO IS ISRAEL?

On each of his visits to the United States, David Ben-Gurion brought a simple and a single message: " Come to the State of Israel. Those of you who wish to fulfill yourselves as Jews, those of you to whom Jewishness is significant, come and settle in our ancestral land."

What Ben-Gurion offered was quite palpable. He held out to American Jews the possibility of living in a community where almost everyone is a Jew and where Jewish life is culturally predominant. Children learn Hebrew as naturally as they grow. The Bible is a school textbook and a national craze. Schools and factories close not only for the Sabbath and the High Holy Days but in celebration of every Jewish holiday. In short, it is an atmosphere in which by simply living in one's neighborhood and being concerned with issues that confront the community one is already involved in Jewish affairs. Here is normal, natural Jewishness, without the strain, the unnatural tension that characterizes the effort to be a Jew in the Diaspora.

Yet implicit in this call are several critical questions: Who really is " Israel "? What are the Jews? Where may true Jewishness be lived?

It was not by chance that the founders of the Jewish State in what was once called " Palestine " chose as its name " Israel," or, as the proclamation of independence sometimes also terms it, " the State of Israel " — the ambiguity is important. But is Israel primarily that political entity which exists today on the soil of what was once called Palestine? The word " Israel," at least for many centuries, had no political connotations. To this day when Jews rise to say the Shema, " Hear, O Israel " — and that is the point at which the word most impressively comes into their lives — they are not calling to a state. They mean the Jewish people as a whole united by its relationship to God: " Adonai, our God, Adonai is One." Of course, the address is to all Jews wherever they may be, and it in some strange way reaches back to all the generations of Jews who were (who found and bequeathed to them this " our " God) and to all the Jews who will yet be (who must carry on this relationship through history to its Messianic consummation). Still, what binds them together as Israel in this moment is that they are united in their loyalty to this God and bound together by faithfulness to his service. That, at least, would seem to be the communal implications of the Shema over the centuries.

From Ben-Gurion and the classical Zionist's point of view, Israel is the Jewish people centered around its State, in its land. Jewishness, therefore, is sharing in the life of that people, now happily revivified and restored in the full dimensions of land, language, and political form. The logical deduction from this point of view is indeed Ben-Gurion's invitation. A full Jewish life can be lived only on the land and in the State — and Jews who have merited reaching this happy day in Jewish history should take advantage of an opportunity denied their ancestors for centuries.

But are all Jews prepared to say that the State of Israel is the one authentic representation of the people of Israel? Is the State by virtue of being a state thereby the embodiment of everything the people has wanted to be and thus the State is, in effect, more important than the people?

Jewish history itself would raise these questions even if Diaspora Jews did not. Are, then, the past two thousand years of Jewish struggle and suffering, of creativity and consecration, relatively insignificant? Were the Jews of those years, most of whom did not live in that land and did not speak its language, not authentically Jewish? Should one dismiss as Jewishly stunted and deprived the Golden Age both of Eastern and Western Islam with its giants such as Saadia and Maimonides? Were Babylonia, Franco-Germany, and Poland not truly Jewish in their varying communal cultural expressions?

Logic would require Ben-Gurion to deprecate these epochs, and he has not flinched from doing so. He has said that the current generation of Israelis has more in common with what the Israelites felt at the time of Joshua than it has with the Jews of the past two thousand years. Although Diaspora Jews can appreciate the new aliveness of the people's ancient entry into the Land, they equally affirm the enduring relevance of a Talmud written in Babylonian Aramaic or Hasidic tales told in Yiddish. It is difficult to believe that as the generations go by, scholars and even ordinary Jews living in the State of Israel will not study the products of Diaspora Jewry and find them not just the archaeological remains of truncated Jewish living but meaningful expressions of Jewishness that still speak to them. The key issue is continuity of spirit. The social setting of Jews has changed radically and with it personal attitudes, but is there no extension of Jewish ideas and values into the modern day? Is the only bond between the generations one of biology, language, and attachment to a land? When the Israelis no longer feel the need to assert their independence against their recent Diaspora past, they will surely recognize that there was an authentic Jewish existence not only outside the Land but in languages other than Hebrew as well.

Two thousand years of Jewish experience have demonstrated to Diaspora Jews the possibility, indeed the desirability, of Jewishness outside the Land. Although today's new freedoms pose special problems in Jewish living — yet simultaneously make available unparalleled opportunities — the past indicates to those who do not immigrate to the State of Israel that their position has solid Jewish precedent and legitimacy.

A thoughtful approach to their attitude would be to examine

how Jewish tradition itself conceived of the Jews. Of course, the
source material is " biased." It is all religious and therefore understands the Jews in this context. But the very word " religious "
needs to be understood in its unique Jewish connotation. The tradition depicts the Jews in their beginnings as a people like other
peoples. They are described in a way that the modern eye recognizes without hesitation as a Semitic group like so many others in
the ancient Near East. As time passes they are subjected to the
same vicissitudes as are other peoples and are with equal effect
buffeted by the customary forces of history. They have normal
difficulties in establishing their monarchy, seeing it break up, being subjugated by larger powers, feeling the impact of economies
expanding and contracting. They are surely nothing like a church
in this period. They are in terms of their social identity a folk, an
ethnic entity, a land-language-literature-destiny group like so
many others in human history.

One thing, however, is different about them and that difference
is decisive, even socially. This people had the good fortune to find
God or to be found by him. Not a god, but God — the one and
only God was its God. No other people had ever so plainly come
to know him. The impact of this new human experience was determinative for the character of this folk and it has been influenced by this discovery/revelation ever since.

One cannot limit the impact of this experience to Moses and
the Hebrews traveling through the wilderness. After Moses a prophetic tradition arose that continued not for a few generations
but for centuries. New voices spoke in a fresh way, yet evoking
the same original depth of divine understanding found earlier in
the Mosaic leadership. Equally incredible, though the voices were
often critical, the people accepted their instruction. Thus, over
the centuries the life and character of the Jewish people changed.
What had begun as a people rather like all other peoples had become different from all other peoples; it was the only people whose
peoplehood was determined by its knowledge of God. The tradition says that what gave the Jewish people this unique character
was its relationship with God. This it called the *brit*, the Cove-

nant, the promise, the pledge, the pact between God and this people, made at Sinai and renewed in succeeding generations.

For its part, the Hebrew folk pledged itself to remember God and serve him through all of history by making his law the basis of its life. It might do what every other people does in history — work, marry, create, migrate — but in and through and underneath the life of all mankind was its unique folk dedication — the service of God in loyalty to an ancient pledge. Its purpose was to remind all mankind of him until they came to know him too, to acknowledge him as their God and to live by his law. In turn, they knew God would protect and watch over them. Eventually, he would vindicate its service " in the end of days." This was not an all-encompassing guarantee. Individual Jews, families, or even communities might suffer and die, but the people would survive. Its purpose would ultimately be fulfilled in an era of peace, justice, and love; then they and their patient, obedient faithfulness through all history would be fulfilled.

The people of this Covenant is Israel. It is always truly Israel whenever it lives up to its obligations under that Covenant. Israel is simply the people of that Covenant.

That is the traditional sense of the nature of Israel, expressed in modern language to be sure, but with some variation a widely held affirmation even in modern Judaism. This is the special sense of the word " religious " when applied to Jews. It necessarily has a double meaning — folk and faith, community and Covenant, people and pledge. It must not disturb Jews that Protestantism and Catholicism do not know this intimate fusion of people and religion. The history of religions knows many other social forms for organizing religious groups, as for example, the different structures of Buddhism or Hinduism. Jews have no reason in advance to reject their own. Indeed, without it they could not have survived as they did, nor yet hope to fulfill the Covenant in history. For ethnicity is a strong armor against the destructive forces of history. Its multiple bands have bound this people closely together through the ages and thus kept them loyal. Even today, when belief is modest, what exists is reinforced by the folk feelings. Where there is little or no faith, the ethnic ties still keep many true to their people — hopefully until that day when they or their descendants will find their way back to faith in God and their Covenant with him.

Contrast this view with that held by Ben-Gurion. By his standards, strictly interpreted, it would be possible to have an " Israel " which claimed to be the heartland of all the Jewish people and which at the same time might be completely atheistic. This is no idle fancy. The overwhelming majority of Israelis today are not religious in the generally accepted sense of the term. Most feel no particular attachment to the European-style Orthodox Judaism which is almost their only religious option. Since their Jewishness is national, they do not feel any special need to be Jews by faith or religious practice. It is not too farfetched to inquire whether, according to Ben-Gurion, conversions to Christianity would still leave their Jewishness unimpaired. As the case of Brother Daniel made clear, even for a secular Jewish state and its law, conversion to Christianity makes one not fully a Jew. The State of Israel may not identify Jewishness with religiosity, but even it had to admit that a rejection of Jewish faith for another religion makes one somehow less a Jewish national. That clash of sentiment with philosophy was quite revealing.

Clearly, Israel cannot even largely be identified with a particular state. Israel must rather be understood as the community of the Covenant wherever it is and under whatever circumstances, though it becomes most clearly visible when it is living a self-determining existence on its homeland.

The historical origins of the present religious/secular split may help us understand its implications better. The emancipation from the ghetto brought this unique and bewildering division upon Jewish life. Before it, there was no distinction between what it meant to be a member of the people and at the same time to take on its religious commitment. Every Jew was a Jew by relation to God and a member of the Jewish people simultaneously. Since his admittance to the modern world the Jew has faced the problem of identifying himself in some form which is deemed both modern and acceptable in terms of contemporary political and social structures. The Jews of the Western world, living in secular states where religion because of its pluralism was a private matter, identified themselves as another religion. Thus they found a safe social place for themselves which they and their neighbors could accept. So to be a Jew today in one of the Western democracies is commonly understood to be a member of a religious group.

The Jews of Central and Eastern Europe could not follow this path. Their emancipation had to take a different form because of their states and their religious leadership. Their countries tended toward religious uniformity with a close tie between church and state. Hence, religious change and development was not tolerated. Moreover, their rabbinate was strongly entrenched and opposed to any change. However, there were many nationality groups in these countries, each with its own culture. The Jews therefore began to identify themselves as a distinct nationality, a group united by land, language, and ethos. In a nationality one might be religious if one wanted — a concession to Jewish history and practice but one that limited the power of the rabbis to impede progress to their own, now small, domain. The dominant factor in being a Jew was being born into the Jewish nation-group and participating in its culture. As other nationalities were in the late nineteenth century moving to rebuild their lives on their land, so should the Jewish people. It was a dynamic forward-looking, self-respecting view.

Yet out of these accomplishments was born a deep and unfortunate cleavage of self-understanding among contemporary Jews. It was almost forced upon them by the differing social circumstances in which they found themselves. It determines, in large part, the confusion in communication between the American Jewish community and its Israeli brothers. The one thinks of the Jews largely in religious terms, the other in a secular perspective. Since Ben-Gurion's position has been clarified, let us follow the issue through from the Diaspora point of view.

If the Jews are the Covenant people, how can Jews of that faith understand the Jewish validity and the significance of the political

entity called the State of Israel? To begin with, the Covenant belief should provide direct religious motivation to be a Zionist. The
oldest, most authentic form of living out the Covenant was to set
up one's own community on one's own land, establishing a society
that would show God's rule in action and thereby be a model and
a sign to the rest of mankind. That, after all, is what the Torah
directs the Jews to do.

Today, in the State of Israel, there is a magnificent possibility
of living out the Covenant, unequaled by anything Jews have
known for nearly two millennia. A Jew who is deeply concerned
about his Jewish religious responsibilities might very well feel he
ought to spend his life participating in the creation of that in-
digenous Covenant community of which so much of the Bible
speaks. Here every aspect of society — its taxes, its education, its
welfare, its foreign aid — is " Jewish," and Jewish values are not
restricted to a carefully delimited and peripheral realm of life.
There is thus not only good reason for building, supporting, and
strengthening the State of Israel but there is also motivation for
immigration as well. Ben-Gurion is, even from the religious standpoint, not unreasonable. But if the Covenant is the criterion of
Jewishness, then much more must be said.

Under the Covenant it may be highly desirable that the Jews
build a state, but that is surely not its fulfillment. The Covenant
calls the Jews not merely to be a people like all other peoples but
one with a messianic task. Ben-Gurion accepts this messianic obligation and often speaks of it. To him it would be in a humanistic
demythologization the end result of the fusion of Hebraic ethics
with Greek science. Here his nationalism still retains signs of its
religious origins. Those who do not share his East European roots
in an observant community or are more rigorous in their secular
redefinition of Jewish peoplehood do not speak in such terms.
Thus no voices rise from other leaders in the State of Israel, most
conspicuously not from the younger ones, that messianism is indeed their people's task. With the Covenant as the standard,
there is, in a way, less Jewishness to be found in such a " normal-

ized " State of Israel than in an " abnormal " Diaspora existence whose communities accepted the religious commitments of the Jewish people. When the State of Israel seeks to be Zion, when nationalism becomes indeed Zionism in the prayer book's centuries-old, hallowed, messianic sense, then it evokes and commands a special sense of Jewish respect and concern.

This is the continuing contribution that the faithful Diaspora Jew can make to his Israeli brother. He can remind him of the religious roots from which they both sprang, of that transcendent other part of their heritage which he may be forgetting. Out of the spiritual experience of the Diaspora communities, both failures and successes, can come a uniquely helpful strength and encouragement to those groups within the State which seek in their own way to develop the religious spirit implicit there.

That hope for the religious development of the State of Israel is rooted in its special national character. How long can a people read and cherish the Bible and remain fully secular? To be vitally concerned with the prophetic imperatives, their standards of righteousness and their demands for justice, means sooner or later coming to wonder why. When a people is willing to sacrifice to bring in its brothers from all over the world, to subject itself to all forms of austerity to feed its hungry, clothe its naked, plead mercy for the refugee widow, seek justice for the displaced orphan, such a people, wittingly or not, is close to the God of the Bible. Is it, then, too much to hope that when the pressures of building and defending the State give way, the grandchildren may reclaim the traditions the parents rejected?

The most important because the most positive point still remains to be made. Life in the State of Israel is not the only genuine way of expressing the Covenant or of living by it.

The last two thousand years of Jewish history, seen in proper focus, testify that there are indeed other and varied modes of being an authentic Jew. In many geographic, political, and social circumstances Jews have found it possible to live by the Covenant and thus to be recognizably and legitimately Jewish. While the emancipation has made it difficult to be truly a Jew, it has not made it impossible.

How extraordinary a prospect would open up if American Jews, now groping for a sense and style of Jewish living, accepted as basic to their life the premise that they are indeed the inheritors of this ancient promise! What if, like other generations in the past, American Jews would pledge themselves in their affluent, secular society to the task that their people have carried on historically? If ever an effective nucleus of American Jews would recognize this as their responsibility, if they would commit their means, their leisure, their intelligence, the power that their talent and industry has won them, could they not build a Jewish community as true to the Covenant as any other the Jewish tradition has yet known? To be sure, it would be expressed in forms somewhat different from those which Jews have used before, for no Jewry has ever been in the open, participating situation of American Jews.

The risks are real and great but so are the possibilities. It is clear that American Jews live in a predominantly Christian culture, and find it necessary to explain, to defend, to reexamine their faith and culture against those of the outside world. This may lead to doubt and to disbelief, even to humanistic dissociation, but it also tends to produce a whole realm of philosophy and willed practice which reveals new dimensions and depths in the old Judaism. Thus, in being part of the most technically advanced civilization known to mankind, the new Judaism must come to grips with the moral problems that society is creating for man, most notably his dehumanization. The Diaspora Jews are, so to speak, the spiritual advance guard of the people making its way through history and by their wide dispersion another hope for its historic continuity.

So though it is vitally important to have a Jewish state seeking its own roots, building its own culture, and holding high the standard of Jewish self-determination, it is also desirable, perhaps even necessary, to have another pole — Jews who live outside the State of Israel, who establish Jewish outposts in the great cultures and societies, who must therefore ever seek to understand the implications of Israel's Covenant in new terms to meet the new conditions.

The Jews in the small Land of Israel will benefit by the cross-fertilization of ideas and concepts from those Jews who willingly take a precarious stand on the periphery so that they may transmit the lessons learned while participating in the forward-driving movements of human history. As these Diaspora Jews face the danger of being lost in their great societies, of bartering away their Jewishness for supposed gains, they can be reminded by that center in the State of Israel of what Jewish knowledge and Jewish self-respect imply.

Is it too much to believe that there are two ways of living out the Covenant, each legitimate, each facing certain risks, each capable of contributing to the other in such a way that Judaism can be fructified?

Jewish optimism born of millennia of transcending historical realism says it is not. If American Jewry can produce the kind of Jew who accepts the Covenant as his own and is willing to help build a community in that understanding, then the most important contribution such a Jew can make to the State of Israel and, more important by far, to the God of Israel, whom they both should serve, is to make Judaism alive and vital and significant right where he is.

Chapter

6

JUDAISM AND THE SECULAR STATE

The traditional Jewish attitude toward states is inevitably dialectical. It cannot be categorically propositional, for Biblical Judaism affirms fundamentally both that God is the undisputed Sovereign of all creation and that he fulfills his sovereignty in human history through individual men and social institutions (without thereby infringing on man's freedom). The first belief sets limits to the authority of human governments; the second authorizes them.

The universality of God's sovereignty in early Israelite belief is still a matter of debate among students of the Bible. Minimalist estimates concede only that he was already in the days of the Judges the exclusive God of the Hebrew people; others now argue that Hebrew monotheism originated with the patriarchs.[1] More important is the dimensional question. This God, apparently from the earliest days, has transcended nature and may not be identified with anything in it. That is in many ways his most characteristic attribute. It gives rise to the unrelenting fight against idolatry which some consider central to the Biblical experience.[2] It is equally the source of that other unprecedented Biblical passion, that human kings are themselves fully subject to God's law. They may not, as in other nations, seek to identify themselves with God himself, nor insist that what they do is necessarily his will. The seer-prophet, who authenticates the Hebrew monarchy and in increasing glory, until its disastrous end, stands over against it in judgment and rebuke, is the incarnation of God's claim to undivided ultimate loyalty.[3]

No wonder, then, that when the Hebrews request a king, God is heard to say, " They have rejected me from being king over them " (I Sam. 8:7). God alone should be the Hebrews' immediate ruler as he was in the wilderness or in the period of early settlement when he raised up occasional leaders to serve his purposes in times of crisis. To impose a lasting human government between the ruling, transcendent God and his people seemed blasphemy. That sense of limit to man's self-government is surely at the heart of this classic chapter. It is so much a continuing reality in Jewish religious thought that centuries later, after the exile, it reappears in Ezra's validation of Jewish existence without political autonomy as already evidenced in the changes made in Zechariah's proclamation to Zerubbabel.[4] There, too, the ideal Israelite king, the Messiah, is not an autonomous *Übermensch*, but a man who rules in God's name to effect God's law. God alone is truly King, Sovereign, Governor.

Yet the other side of the covenantal understanding of religion is also affirmed. Though God is transcendent, he is not normally withdrawn from his creation. He cares for it and participates in it. He guides it in revelation, redirects it in justice, and preserves it in love, awaiting with infinite patience and understanding its ultimate free acceptance of his rule and, thus, the full establishment of his Kingdom. He is, therefore, intimately involved with marriages and inheritance, with slavery and the stranger, with priests and seers, and thus ultimately with kings. They are the very stuff of history in which his sovereignty must be made manifest. The author of I Samuel attributes the Israelite call for a human king to the people's baseness, in itself a human historical reality not to be ignored. The modern mind cannot help noting that a crisis had arisen which made the inherited social structure unworkable. In the face of Philistine military organization and technology, a divided Israel could not long survive. If Israel now insisted on maintaining forms of social cooperation suited to a previous period, when foes were few and temporary, it would die at the hand of a persistent, powerful Philistine people. But — for God's sake — Israel must survive! It exists not for itself or for the moment, but as God's instrument for the transformation of all human history! It must wait and work in history until the Messiah comes. To withdraw from history by suicide or social paralysis would be to deny its Covenant root and branch. Thus Samuel learned what later Jewish sages institutionalized, that in the face of social change God will teach Israel how it may find the new forms which will enable it to continue to serve him amid the realities of history. In this case, he unexpectedly permits a king, providing, to be sure, that this new social structure not be construed as any diminishment of God's real if ultimate sovereignty over this people. In succeeding centuries, his Torah tradition, progressively developed by the rabbis, will be the continuing medium of reconciling the simultaneous demands of his rule and Israel's need to serve him in history.[5] Thus, in a word, governments are authorized, but only conditionally.

The Jewish tradition views the account of First Samuel as the adumbration of the Mosaic commandment to appoint a king (Deut. 17:14-15). The interpretation accorded these authoritative verses by the classic rabbinic texts illustrates well the fundamental dialectic being described here. Because the Deuteronomic wording exhibits the ambiguity typical of much Biblical formulation, the Tannaitic commentators (pre-200 of the Common Era) are divided as to whether the appointment of a king over Israel was obligatory or optional. Their positions, theologically, are but another form of the Biblical dialectic.[6] These differences were already reflected in the Hellenistic Jewish thinkers of the first century. Philo, reflecting the Greek philosophic concern for proper political organization, apparently believed monarchy a Mosaic mandate.[7] Josephus, whose background was aristocratic and Boethusian/Sadducean, follows the latter's predilection for a priestly, theocratic rule and therefore considers the text only permission, not a religious requirement.[8] To all these Jewish thinkers, the question posed live political options. When two Judean revolutions failed and time passed, it became increasingly hypothetical. When no normal historical ruler seemed imminent for the Jewish people, Jewish politics became almost completely eschatological. That, it seems to me, explains why the monarchists gained the ascendancy, since all discussions of a Jewish king were now conducted in the context of waiting for the promised Son of David.

Thus almost all medieval Jewish comment on this question is to the effect that the establishment of a Jewish monarchy is obligatory. Maimonides lists it as one of the 248 positive commandments [9] and the *Sefer Hachinuch* specifies it as one of the duties incumbent upon the Jewish people.[10] Such major intellectual and legal figures of the thirteenth and fourteenth centuries as Nachmanides, Moses of Coucy, Gersonides, and Bachya ben Asher may be mentioned as sharing this position.[11] By contrast, only two dissenting authorities can be cited.

Abraham Ibn Ezra, commenting on the Deuteronomic provision, regards it as an option, but we are unable to tell whether his comment has more than grammatical significance. Only Isaac Abravanel presents a major argument against having a Jewish king.[12] His position almost certainly derives from his experience as a statesman and practicing politician and is focused upon immediate historic reality. Having served under several monarchs (always with tragic result) and having been influenced by the Christian and humanist political thought of his day (unlike his Jewish philosophical predecessors), Abravanel revives the antimonarchic arguments of the Books of Samuel. He is too much a realist to believe that men in sinful history can actually be ruled by God directly. Rather, he considers monarchy a form of government inferior to what might be called a democracy of the elite.[13] That is the best hope of doing God's will until the Messiah comes, for he alone can be a king pleasing in God's sight.

Abravanel, commenting on the law of the Torah for Jewish states, is undoubtedly thinking of what it may teach non-Jewish governments. Yet Deuteronomic law is not addressed to the nations of the world, but only to Israel. Does the inner tension it knows between the divine and Jewish kings extend to non-Jewish kings ruling over a non-Jewish state? Though there is little generalized opinion available on this topic, the answer may be ventured with some confidence that the same basic dialectic holds true.[14] It may most conveniently be exposed by a consideration of the attitudes clustering around the concepts *dina d'malchuta dina*[15] and *galut*.

The Amoraic master Samuel enunciated the principle *dina d'malchuta dina*, "the law of the [non-Jewish ruler of the] land is the law [for Jews]," early in the third century in Parthia (Babylonia), and it became an accepted legal norm for succeeding Jewish law and thought.[16] Samuel was referring only to non-Jewish legal procedures, such as witnesses and documents, but the sense of his pronouncement must be seen as far more inclusive. By the third century, Jewish life in the Land of Israel was in serious decline both as to numbers and in communal vitality. The spiritual strength of Judaism was to be found in communities widely scattered through the Roman and — more influentially — the Parthian empires. If Israel was to survive amid the realities of human affairs as God's witness, it had to find a social pattern other than independent national existence on its own land to make that service of endurance possible. Moreover, it had to be as authentic to Israel's messianic purpose in history as it was useful to its survival.

All this was implied in Samuel's dictum. The Jew could bind himself to the civil law of the land in which he found himself as part of his Covenant with God. He therefore could be loyal to his non-Jewish king even as he remained loyal to God in his relationship to him. Though no Talmudic references are made to it, the modern mind sees here the recapitulation of the message Jeremiah sent centuries earlier to that same Babylonian Jewry: "Seek the welfare of the city where I have sent you into exile, and pray to the LORD on its behalf, for in its welfare you will find your welfare" (Jer. 29:7). This passage may be called the charter of authenticity for Diaspora forms of covenantal existence.

Samuel's principle, affirming the religious legitimacy of non-Jewish governments and their rights, is not without limits in its development in later Jewish law. Two qualifications are relevant to the question of the general Jewish attitude toward non-Jewish states. If the king acts in an arbitrary and capricious fashion, such as taxing one group of citizens or one province in a way incommensurate with what he has demanded of others, then his decrees are not considered binding by Jewish law; they are *dina d'malka,* "the king's law," rather than *dina d'malchuta,* "the law of the kingdom." The other case is more obvious. The authority of the non-Jewish king does not extend to more strictly religious matters, such as what is ritually clean or unclean, permitted or forbidden. What Judaism seeks in non-Jewish governments is obviously God's righteousness fulfilled. According to Jewish law, the sons of Noah (that is, all men) are commanded by God to be just to one another. Thus the non-Jewish king is obligated to establish justice and authorized when he does so. Therefore, the Jew has a religious basis for his civil responsibility to such a non-Jewish king. The fuller obedience to God would, of course, be for Israel to live as a community whose life was structured by God's Torah. The non-Jewish world is not commanded by and does not observe that fuller law. Hence, life for the Jew in the midst of a nonobservant people can never have the same quality of sanctity that independent life on its own land might have. That is the source of the negative religious attitudes toward non-Jewish states and they may best be analyzed in terms of the concept *galut.*

Galut may be translated "exile," but the political and geographic connotations of that English term are misleading.

Since the Biblical God is the God of history, politics and geography can be religious matters to Judaism. God grants a land to his people as part of their Covenant and he makes their continued happy existence on that land contingent upon their observance of his commandments. God authorizes a king for them as noted, but he and they are expected to be no less observant of God's behest because of it; when they are, God's prophets warn both king and people that God will exile them in payment for their sins. Thus *galut* is fundamentally a theological category.[17] It testifies to Israel's past infidelity and her present punishment, for

that is what life under a non-Jewish government is when compared to full covenantal existence on one's promised land under
the divine law. And as centuries went by and the experience of
cruel and oppressive monarchs multiplied, the sense of *galut* deep-
ened and messianic expectation grew more fervent. How soon this
concept was applied to God himself — that God had become an
alien in creation — is difficult to say, but early in the Common
Era Israel's political-geographic-religious situation was seen as a
symbol of God's own alienation, and the hope of Israel's restora-
tion to its land under its messianic king became inextricably identified with the return of God's presence to the world and the full
establishment of his Kingdom. That is why the religious Jew will
still be able to say, much to the consternation of the Israeli na-
tionalist, that the State of Israel itself is *galut*. Zionist theoreticians
in their thoroughgoing political secularization of traditional Jewish
religious concepts transvalued *galut* into simple geographic exile.
For them, therefore, to return to the Land of Israel and live as
part of the State of Israel is the end of exile.[18] What a warning
this should sound in the ears of those who are eager to give secular, particularly political, interpretations of traditional religious
concepts, for the present State of Israel in this Zionist system becomes the answer to centuries of Jewish prayer for the end of exile
and the resolution of the mysteries of the people of Israel's millennial service! The religious Jew, however, knows that the real
galut is metaphysical and so cannot end until God manifests his
Kingdom. For him the State of Israel is at best, as the mystics put
it, *atchalta d'g'ula*, "the beginning of redemption," and, as we
shall see below, he is therefore preserved from jingoism and un-
critical nationalism. Rather, he must judge that state as he judges
other states, by the prophetic criterion of its fulfillment of God's
law.[19]

The dialectical "Yes"/"No" of Judaism toward non-Jewish
kings took a radical shift in the direction of an almost unqualified "Yes" with the rise of modern democracy and the secular
state. Where there had been for centuries only Zoroastrian, Muslim, or Christian governments, now there was to be a government

that was not directly concerned with religion. Political loyalty was one thing, religious commitment another. The state cared only about good citizenship; religion was in effect a private decision removed from the public domain. Because the non-Jewish state no longer held a religion antagonistic to Judaism, because it had no religion at all but was secular, the Jew could be a part of it, and equal in its midst.[20] Indeed, for the first time it became his state as much as anyone else's.

No wonder the Jews hailed Napoleon with messianic fervor and gladly rushed from their enforced segregation to share a new life.[21] Much of the history of nineteenth- and twentieth-century European and American Jewry may be read as one continuing fight to find ways to win in practice the opportunities promised in this emancipation. In some countries democracy was largely fraudulent, and Jewish rights never became widely meaningful. In others it provided a measure of opportunity rarely equaled in the history of the Jewish dispersion. The newness of the gift of freedom and the continuing effort to expand and safeguard it still set the dominant tone of Jewish life and thought in the United States. This may be somewhat more sophisticated today than in the days of mass immigration and frenzied acculturation, but with the overwhelming number of American Jews only three generations away from the degradation of the *shtetl*, the East European Jewish village, equality is still too fresh to be taken for granted by most American Jews.

That mood of euphoric acceptance and wholehearted commitment lies behind the virtual absence of *galut* concepts from the religious thought of Jews in democratic countries in the past century or so.[22] By comparison to the oppression of religious governments, the tolerance created by secular governments seemed in effect an end to *galut*. Nothing made Zionist theoreticians (largely East Europeans) of the late nineteenth and early twentieth centuries more unpopular with their Western brothers than their assertion that Jews would never fully be accepted in modern democracies and needed a country of their own. Nor did the Jewish masses of Europe accept the argument, for they directed their migration in overwhelming numbers to the United States, and only the later immigration laws and Hitlerian conquests made the Land of Israel their personal goal. The metaphysical conception of *galut* similarly had little meaning for them when contrasted with a country whose streets, rumor said, were paved with gold and whose social and economic opportunities proved realistically far greater than any Jewish immigrant to these shores could have anticipated. Compared to the grim poverty and human misery of life in Eastern Europe, America seemed too much like the answer to a prayer to be considered exile. The Jew has had a rapturous love affair with America, and it has made him almost unable to say " No " to her.

Yet the time has clearly come to reassert the negative side of the dialectical Jewish view of states. In part this is motivated by the profound general sense of personal alienation which marks so much of the criticism of contemporary society. For the believing Jew it is the duty deriving from his affirmation of the Covenant. To take God and his demands seriously provides a perspective in which even the best of secular, democratic welfare states is not nearly good enough. To wait and work for the Kingdom of God requires a renewed commitment to the concept of *galut* in all its theopolitical depth.

This is a matter of particular urgency because the contemporary nation-state is the closest thing to an effective absolute that modern man knows. The totalitarian states are only a dramatic example of what seems to be happening wherever governments organize and, in the name of efficiency, centralize. Let the needs of the state become paramount, as in a war, and the almost unqualified nature of its power and the absence of any significant right greater than its self-preservation are made abundantly clear. No wonder Orwell could predict that the normal political situation in 1984 would be continual war! So, too, where states agree to join in international parliament, their sovereignty in internal affairs must be guaranteed them, with some countries even being granted a veto over the will of the entire body.

As the democratic state has effectively made its rights increasingly paramount, so it has moved to neutralize or control all potential rivals for social power. It does this not as in the days of tyranny by proscription or persecution, but more dangerously by paternalism and patronage. Who then can stand up to so beneficent a Federal Government? States' rights means little in the face of necessary federal aid; independent capitalism is a fantasy exploded by nonlegislated economic guidelines and luscious defense contracts; academic autonomy walks a cliff edge, lured below by research grants and building loans; now artists of every variety are to benefit from government largesse. The next step, one may be certain, will be fellowships to stimulate protests and dissent. Economic determinism aside, when one's mouth is full of gravy, it is difficult to cry out.

The threat of government without significant opposition will hardly be affected by American politics or secular morality. Since World War II, Americans have shown themselves substantially unwilling to commit themselves to any large-scale political ideology that might make radical criticism of government a necessity. Perhaps no more than a minority of Americans ever was active politically, but there was always hope that the creative few might change social policy. Hot politics, except for some few specific face-to-face issues, is out of place in a world seeking to play it cool. Passionate conviction is even less evident as an effective offset to governmental self-aggrandizement. Affluence has had its dulling effect on individuals as on institutions. Most Americans could define the immediate good as being left alone by the government to enjoy what they have, or perhaps as being given a little more. The morality of privatism may make for better families and friendships, but its foundation is withdrawal from responsibility for politics and history.

The issue becomes more painfully difficult as the state takes on what must be termed a new and broader ethical responsibility. Today it seeks to fulfill many of the injunctions the Bible taught that God demanded of his people. Moreover, it does its work of righteousness in a technically competent, full-scale outreach, whereas the religions operated, at best, with great spirit but also in a piecemeal, frequently ineffectual fashion. By finding work for the poor, teaching the illiterate, housing the dispossessed, healing the sick, dignifying the elderly (throughout the world!), the United States Government may claim a certain religious merit. How easy, then, for the state to excuse its other failings by the goodness it does! How soon a little righteousness becomes a general justification, and like the bad Pharisees and impious Christians of every generation, even what little was good now becomes an instrument of self-delusion and thus moral perversion! Niebuhr's burden concerning immoral societies joined to Acton's confession of the teleology of power should at this late date free us sufficiently from our illusions to see that the very good the state does demands more than the religious " Yes "; it demands religion's watchful and chastening " No."

Religion is the major remaining social body that has hope, as long as it maintains its loyalty to a transcendent God, of standing over against the government and its idolatrous self-seeking. Every alliance with or dependence upon the government it allows weakens the possibility of its fulfilling that critical role. To put it less socially and more theologically, as it serves God, religion must criticize government, particularly where the state seeks to supplant or ignore him, and the more a religion relies on government, the less it will be able to remain faithful to its primary tasks, to serve him before all else.

Israel's prophets may serve as the classic example of this truth.[23] As long as they were hirelings — royal seers and diviners — the men of God could in rare instances only, as Samuel, Nathan, and Elijah did, rise to the heights of later prophecy. Perhaps of that latter group Isaiah was part of the establishment. If so, he is an even greater genius than men have thought. It is only when the herdsman is taken from the sheep, almost against his will, and the unknown Amos confronts the professional visionary Amaziah in the royal sanctuary, that prophecy reaches classic proportions. The vicissitudes of Israel's prophets, loners almost to a man, are proof of the stand one must be ready to take and the cost one must be ready to pay to bring God's judgment to bear on society even when one stands in the midst of a people covenanted to him. How much more is this the case in the secular state! This is not to argue that the sole function of religion in modern America is prophetic criticism. There is ample room for the appreciation of what the state has and can continue to do, for the religious " Yes." Yet that is the easy word in a day of politics by consensus and social manipulation by human relations techniques. Religion will be most true to itself today as the home of all those alienated ultimately from any government but the Kingdom of God, and therefore uniquely valuable to American democracy as the institutionalization of the principle and practice of social judgment and dissent.

NOTES: *Chapter 6*

1. So Theodore Robinson can write, " Such doctrines as those of Amos and Isaiah must lead *in the long run* to a pure monotheism " (A *History of Israel* [Oxford University Press, 1932], Vol. I, p. 407, emphasis added). The discussion by Gerhard von Rad is far more tempered but essentially skeptical of early monotheism (*Old Testament Theology* [Harper & Row, Publishers, Inc., 1962], pp. 210 ff.). E. A. Speiser's revisionism gives vigor to the more traditional position (*Genesis*, Vol. I of *The Anchor Bible*, ed. by William F. Albright and David N. Freedman [Doubleday & Company, Inc., 1964], pp. xlv ff.).

2. " The dominant tenet of Hebrew thought is the absolute transcendence of God. Yahweh is not in nature." This, by contrast to Mesopotamian and Egyptian thought, is the summary of H. and H. A. Frankfort *et al.*, in *Before Philosophy* (Pelican Books, 1946), p. 241. Walther Eichrodt links this emphasis on transcendence with the sense of His immanence, though that is a different thing from being " in nature " (*Theology of the Old Testament* [The Old Testament Library, Vol. I; The Westminster Press, 1961], p. 205). The centrality of anti-idolatry to Biblical Judaism is itself the dominant motif of Ezekiel Kaufmann's *Toldot Haemunah Hayisraelit* (Dvir, 1937). See the first sentence of Vol. I, Part 1, p. 1.

3. The inner experience is clarified by Robert B. Y. Scott, *The Relevance of the Prophets* (The Macmillan Company, 1944), pp. 52 f. and 106 ff. On the king's role and Israelite law, see Roland de Vaux, *Ancient Israel* (McGraw-Hill Publishing Co., Inc., 1961), pp. 144 ff., especially Sec. 5 on the king's legislative and judicial powers.

4. Robert H. Pfeiffer, *Introduction to the Old Testament* (Harper & Brothers, 1941), pp. 605 f., is more graphic but less detailed than Otto Eissfeldt, *The Old Testament* (Harper & Row, Publishers, Inc., 1965), pp. 430–432.

5. The early statement of R. Travers Herford in *The Pharisees* (The Macmillan Company, 1924), pp. 69 ff., on tradition's supplementing the written Torah remains basically correct. Succeeding scholarship has only extended this insight that law is an adaptive instrument which allows change to enter Judaism without the loss of Judaism's essential character.

6. The same material is given in three places with some variation, none of special conceptual note: *Sifre Dt.*, par. 156, p. 105a; Midrash Tannaim to Dt. 17:14, pp. 103–104; *Sanhedrin* 20b. In the former text, R. Judah, who considers the Deuteronomic injunction mandatory, gives this explanation for what then seems the surprising rebuke of I Sam., ch. 8, viz., they asked for the king at too early a date. The dichotomy of views continues into later rabbinic literature. Positively, one should recite a blessing upon seeing a Jewish king (Ber. 58a); impudence to him is like impudence to God (Gen. Rab. 94); when the people obey their rulers, God does what they decide (Dt. Rab. 1), for even the smallest of appointees has great status — some say he acts with God's authority (R.H. 25b and B.B. 91b); and even the Roman Government might be called "good," for it established justice (Gen. Rab. 9.13). Negatively, many a remark approaching the cynical is recorded with respect to the action of Jewish community officials, even oftener respecting non-Jewish governors. (See P.A. 1.10, Pes. 87b, Tan. Mish. 2, Midrash Hagadol, ed. by Solomon Schechter, p. 412, and Yoma 22b, which notes that Saul's kingdom ended because it was not dishonest!)

7. Philo Judaeus, *De Specialibus Legibus*, IV, 30, 157, *Philo: Foundations of Religious Philosophy in Judaism, Christianity, and Islam*, Harry Austryn Wolfson (Harvard University Press, 1947), Vol. II, p. 329.

8. Josephus, *Contra Apion*, 2.16; *Antiquities*, IV, 8, 17, 223. The interpretation of his Boethusian background is taken from Solomon Zeitlin, *The Rise and Fall of the Judaean State* (The Jewish Publication Society of America, 1967), Vol. II. Simon Federbush contends, however, in *Mishpat Hameluchah Beyisrael* (Mosad Harav Kuk, 1952), pp. 26 f., that Josephus' position on theocracy has been misunderstood and that only later generations ever thought it meant hierocracy, the rule of priests. Jewish faith demands equality for all religions and peoples. Hence religious and political powers were always separated in Israel. The exceptions, the Hasmonaean rulers, were derogated by rabbinic Judaism. His proof, aside from a general statement in the Jerusalem Talmud, is a citation from the thirteenth-century Nachmanides. The ideological intent behind this reconstruction is discussed in n. 13 below.

9. Moses Maimonides, *Sefer Hamitzvot*, positive commandment 173. Note the implicit assumption that the king is expected to follow the Torah to be worthy of preeminence. Monarchy is given a generally Aristotelian justification in *The Guide of the Perplexed*, II, 40. The legal prescriptions are given in *M. T. Hilchot Melachim*. Note that the messianic laws are part of this discussion of Jewish kings (Chs. 11 and 12). See the discussion in Leo Strauss, "Abravanel's Political Theory," *Isaac Abravanel*, ed. by J. B. Trend and H. M. J. Loewe (London: Cambridge University Press, 1937), pp. 106 ff.

10. *Sefer Hachinuch*, par. 497.

11. So states Strauss, in "Abravanel's Political Theory," p. 119, in referring to the Biblical commentaries to Deut. 17:14 f. of the former two. An instructive parallel to the Muslim position is drawn by S. D. F. Goitein in "Attitudes Toward Government in Islam and Judaism," in his *Studies in Islamic History and Institutions* (Leiden: E. J. Brill, 1966). Since the Koran contains no references to political regimes, some authorities could argue that

the Caliphate was not religiously required and no form of political organization is preferable to another. While such arguments were heard when the Caliphate made its appearance, they gradually disappeared in the face of the reality. The matter apparently caused no intellectual concern to later generations, for the topic of monarchy is not dealt with in the later Muslim codes or classic philosophies.

12. Strauss, " Abravanel's Political Theory," is particularly helpful for his study of the context of contemporary political theory in which Abravanel's departure from past theory is best to be understood. A somewhat more detailed discussion of Abravanel's ideas in their development is found in Ben Zion Netanyahu, *Don Isaac Abravanel* (The Jewish Publication Society of America, 1953), pp. 183 ff. His rejection of the influence of contemporary political thought on Abravanel is not convincing to me after Strauss's demonstration.

13. Simon Federbush seizes upon this position as a means of arguing that traditional Jewish law does not require a monarchy and hence the establishment of a democracy in the contemporary State of Israel is fully halachic! His treatment of the prevailing, opposing view may be seen in his comment, " But from the simple meaning of the Torah text it is clear that it is not commanded; and the phrase 'like all the nations' is a clear implication of derogation, which is also clear from the simple meaning of Samuel's reply to those seeking a king " (*Mishpat Hameluchah Beyisrael*, p. 39). He further points out that since there is no prophet or Sanhedrin today to induct and ratify the king, a monarchy is a practical impossibility. The conclusion is, however, made *lefi ruach hatorah* (" according to the spirit of the Torah "), a phrase and concept Federbush would roundly condemn if it were utilized by non-Orthodox interpreters for similar treatments of traditional law to allow for more modern social arrangements (*ibid.*, p. 40).

14. The dialectic developed by Joseph Baer Soloveitchik regarding the two kinds of peoplehood, the one biological and compulsory, the other an especially human response because free, is of a different order. Soloveitchik operates here, characteristically, with

a typology which he uses to understand history but which is not fully reflected in any historical phenomenon. The contrast that he points out is not so much between the rule of God and the rule of men in actual institutions as between the two separate but intertwined modes of Jewish existence as a people — the biological and the theological. They make possible the positive acceptance of the current secular State of Israel but demand an effort to help it live up to its full Jewish character (" Kol Dodi Dofek," *Torah Umeluchah,* ed. by Simon Federbush [Mosad Harav Kuk, 1961], pp. 11–44).

15. An alternate possibility for these positive attitudes may be found in the prohibition against rebellion, the laws of *mored bemalchut.* They are, however, less central to Jewish law, and the attitudes concerning them seem to have developed most clearly at a much later period. See the somewhat abstract discussion by Simon Federbush, *Mishpat Hameluchah Beyisrael,* pp. 84 ff. For a brief description of the legal tradition, see J. D. Eisenstein, art. " Mored Bemalchut," *Otzar Dinim Uminhagim* (Hebrew Publishing Co., 1917), p. 211. I know of no English discussion of this theme. A brief list of *aggadic* passages calling for reverence to kings is given in art. " King," *The Jewish Encyclopedia,* Sec. " In Rabbinical Literature," Vol. VII, p. 502. A more realistic picture of what the average man expects of a king is given in the imaginative contrasts between the immorality of earthly kings and the righteousness of the King of Kings. See the index entry " Earthly Kings " in *A Rabbinic Anthology,* ed. by C. G. Montefiore and H. Loewe (The Macmillan Company, 1938), p. 791.

16. See the discussion of this principle, noteworthy for its full citation of later and occasionally diverging authorities, in the (Hebrew) *Talmudic Encyclopedia* (Jerusalem, 1956), art. " Dina Demalchuta Dina," Vol. VII, cols. 295–308. However, Salo Baron cautions that this principle was never given definitive limits or fully clarified (*The Jewish Community* [The Jewish Publication Society of America, 1942], Vol. II, pp. 216 ff.; *A Social and Religious History of the Jews* [2d ed., Columbia University Press, 1957], Vol. V, pp. 75 ff.). Leo Landman has detailed the legal

situations to which the principle was first applied as well as the
later history of its usage. While he records considerable diversity
in interpretation over the centuries, there seems to be far greater
integrity than Baron's comment might have led one to expect.
(*Jewish Law in the Diaspora: Confrontation and Accommodation*
[Dropsie College for Hebrew and Cognate Learning, 1968.])
Landman's study would be more useful had he not almost exclusively restricted his attention to the relevant Jewish legal texts.
The great virtue of Jacob Neusner's treatment of the origin of the
principle is that it is fully set within what we know of Samuel's
relations with Shapur, the Sassanian ruler. Neusner interprets the
introduction of this rule as " *strictly* political," in contrast to the
rabbis' inner, " religious program." I find these terms and the distinction they imply not fully appropriate to significant Jewish
activities and would prefer to apply the dialectic given in this
article: Jewish politics involves theology as Jewish religion is necessarily historic and political. (Jacob Neusner, *A History of the Jews
in Babylonia* [Leiden: E. J. Brill, 1966], Vol. II, pp. 64–72.)

17. The major study of this concept to date is Yitzchak B. Baer,
Galut (Schocken Books, Inc., 1947), the English translation of a
German text published in the early thirties. Baer's nationalistic
and rationalistic concerns seem to me to constrict his treatment
of what he recognizes as the essentially religious origins and connotations of the concept. Thus there is no discussion of the Biblical concept of *galut*, only a short discussion of the *aggadic* notion
of the exile of God's Indwelling Presence, and only brief mention
of medieval mysticism. Hence, Baer's study cannot be relied upon
for a rounded understanding of this doctrine, particularly from
the standpoint of its meaning and place within the structure of
Jewish faith.

18. For an excellent introduction to Zionist ideology, see Arthur
Hertzberg, *The Zionist Idea* (Doubleday & Company, Inc., 1959).
Of particular interest are the Introduction, which carefully distinguishes between Jewish religious tradition and modern secular
thought, and the selections in Parts 4, 5, and 6. Note that a separate section, and only one at that, is given to religious Zionism

(including, quite properly, Martin Buber). David Ben-Gurion's secular messianism is a particularly interesting effort to blend the two streams from the secular side.

19. A sensitive discussion of this problem is to be found in Ernst Simon, " Are We Israelis Still Jews? " *Commentary*, April, 1953. See also Chapter 5.

20. See the convincing analysis of Arthur Hertzberg, " Church, State and the Jews," *Commentary*, April, 1963.

21. The story of the period is engagingly narrated by Howard M. Sachar, *The Course of Modern Jewish History* (The World Publishing Company, 1958), particularly Ch. III, but *passim*. Napoleon was quite harsh to French Jewry, yet they bore his rigors patiently and then exalted him as the founder of their freedom. The latter was what they found surprising. See the perceptive remarks of Zosa Szajkowski, " Judaic-Napoleonica," *Studies in Jewish Bibliography and Folklore*, June, 1956, p. 108.

22. It is typical of the mood of the times that *The Jewish Encyclopedia* of 1904 treats " Exile " with a brief linguistic note and then refers its readers to articles that deal essentially with the Biblical experience of " Banishment " or " Captivity " (in Babylon) but treats Jews away from the Land of Israel by the neutral term " Diaspora."

23. Note the comment by Harry Orlinsky on the possibilities of Israel's prophets' taking pay (" The Seer in Ancient Israel," *Oriens Antiquus*, Vol. IV, fasc. II [1965], p. 154). Bear in mind too that the entire burden of this study is the uniqueness of Israel's prophets (as contrasted with her seers) in comparison to so-called Prophets seen elsewhere in Near Eastern literature. From a quite different perspective there is the still relevant preachment of Martin Buber in " False Prophets," *Israel and the World* (Schocken Books, Inc., 1948), pp. 113 ff.

Chapter

7

THE LITURGY AND ITS DIFFICULTIES

The forms of communal prayer vary greatly among the religions of mankind. From the formulas accompanying stylized dances to spontaneous shouts and cheers, from quiet utterance at a local shrine to mass pilgrimage and recitation, the patterns differ almost without limit. Though Judaism and its daughter religions may hold similar Biblical views of God, man, and the worshiping community, the character of their divine services may fall anywhere between widely placed poles. Thus the Quaker service has no set liturgy or ritual. The Friends meet at an appointed time and wait in silence for the Inner Light to move them to speak or pray. Whether much is said or little, whether emotion overflows or an unruffled calm is broken occasionally by a simple declaration, makes no difference. The meeting has served its function.

Near the other pole stands the Roman Catholic Mass. Here all is ordered by God through the tradition of the church. The number, style, and color of the vestments for this occasion, the specific psalms and prayers and their sequence, the very gestures of the officiant, all are a fixed part of the only authorized pattern of formally required communal worship.

Each religious group shapes and justifies its service in terms of its faith. The Friends believe God works within the individual. For them, unless they are prompted by an active sense of God's presence within, all words are futile, all gestures in his direction meaningless. Better to sit silently and wait in openness for his stirrings in us than to assault him or demand his gracious presence. Here, the group plays no special role in man's relation to him. It is the useful instrument of mutual help and joint labor, but the Quakers have little doctrine of the church. They work and pray together as little more than an aggregation of individuals faithful to the working of the Inner Light in each of them as in others of previous generations.

The Roman Catholic Church, in substantial contrast, knows and encourages personal piety, but it knows, too, that this must be channeled through the church. The church is no human invention, no mere social instrumentality. God established the church. He did so that through it men might receive his grace and serve his will. The Mass is the service he founded, the medium of his love, and the honoring of his will. No private service of the heart, valuable as it may be, can take the place of the church's celebration of the Mass, nor is the worshiper's personal participation required for its effect. The Mass is God's sacrament and fulfills its function not because of its subjective effect on those attending or on those performing it, but from God's action in it.

Where within the broad spectrum of the possibilities of communal prayer does Jewish worship fall? And what are the religious commitments which gave it this form?

Jewish faith affirms the existence of a living relationship between God and all men, not just the Jews. The covenant God made with Noah and his descendants after the Flood is its classic expression. Noah stands for Everyman, since with him God begins history once again. With the previous wickedness washed away, man receives another opportunity and mandate to serve God in righteousness. In the covenant relationship, God gives man some commandments by which to live (most versions say seven) and God, in turn, promises never to bring another flood to destroy mankind. Since that day men may have willfully rejected or quietly ignored that pact. No matter; the Noahide covenant remains and, the Jew believes, provides a continuing possibility that non-Jews such as Jethro or Balaam may truly know God, that there may be righteous men among the nations who will share in the world to come.

What prayer may mean to all men, as a Jew sees it, can be derived from this fundamental understanding. The covenant with Noah established the reality of man's relation to the one, true God. This gives man the basis, perhaps the right, to worship God. More, a real relationship between man, the creature, and God, the creator, would of itself require man to serve God in worship. So the Jewish tradition regularly understood that one of the Noahide commandments was the worship of God, not of idols. (Not without significance is the fact that the covenant with Noah is made when Noah offers a sacrifice.) It may perhaps be unfair to see in the prohibition against idolatry a mandate to worship God, or in the practice of sacrifice the beginnings of prayer. Whether the act of sacrifice was or was not early accompanied by private prayer is not relevant here. In Noah, Melchizedek, Jethro, and Balaam there is an early Biblical tradition that non-Jews might truly worship God, a tradition which the rabbis centuries later formalized and symbolized in their concept of the covenant of Noah. As prayer accompanied sacrifice in Biblical times and gradually established itself as a separate and legitimate means of Jewish worship, so it is safe to assume a similar legitimacy for the righteous non-Jew. (Solomon's dedication prayer beseeching God's attention to such non-Jewish prayers is a unique Biblical indication. There are a number of positive rabbinic expressions.)

Another aspect of the general view may be derived from the view that all men, not just Jews, were created in the image of God. Man is enough like God to know God exists, to understand what God wants of him, to stand in a covenant with him, and thus to worship him. Man, because he is in essence like God, can and should communicate with his Creator, the Master of the universe in which man lives.

This is a belief about all men and, at the same time, about each man individually. From it, as prayer becomes ever more significant in Judaism, follows an emphasis on the individual. Our earliest information about Jewish prayer services (again foregoing hypotheses concerning the Temple sacrifices and the personal prayers mentioned in the Bible) comes from the first century of the Common Era. In these sources the Jewish prayer service is already determinedly individualistic. Nothing happens in the service which the man who has come to pray does not himself bring about. The fixed order of the prayers, the leadership of respected figures, the communion with neighbors, the special room devoted to the worship of God — all these may help. They may be invaluable to the individual, even humanly indispensable. They remain means, instruments, accessories. They cannot take the place of the individual's own action, his turning to God in attentive respect.

The rabbis called this indispensable personal element of prayer *kavvannah*. They debated to what extent the unlearned and the ill at ease, the simpleminded and the confused, must have *kavvannah* if their service was to fulfill the commandment to pray. Realistic as always, they might reduce the requirement to a heartfelt " Amen " (" So be it " or even " That is what I, too, mean to say ") to the leader's prayer; or to the first sentence of the Sh'ma; or perhaps even to its last word, " One! " Still, these were the *limits*. They were the extremes to which they were willing to go to make regular prayer possible for real men in real history. But beyond this minimum of individual devotion even their realism could not force them to go. Ultimately, the Jewish view of prayer involves an act of the will, a turning of the self. Normally, *kavvannah*, personal involvement and projection, was the standard and the hope of Jewish worship.

Thus, the Jewish service, unlike the Catholic Mass, is never sacramental. God does not so much work through the proper recitation of the liturgy as in free response to it. The Jewish service is precisely a prayer service, an order of petitions, praises, thanksgivings, and acknowledgments which men created for God. Its essential characteristic is address, not persons, acts, or places. Anyone may lead a Jewish service, and Jewish ordination is not required to qualify or consecrate one for this role. No objects are used in the service, though a prayer book will help one to remember the order and wording of the prayers. The service may be held in any reasonably appropriate place. While ten men are required for the full form of worship, the multiplication of one by ten does not suddenly alter their religious significance as individuals; it only makes them formally representative of their community. As far as their worship is concerned, they still depend upon the personal efforts of those present. Unless the congregants pray, regardless of rabbi, cantor, synagogue, or the number present, they have not achieved Judaism's purpose in directing them to assemble for prayer.

The point is important not only as a matter of comparison, but because it is vital in understanding the contemporary ineffectiveness of Jewish worship. The contemporary synagogue in its eagerness to have aesthetically appealing services has largely forgotten the role of the individual worshiper.

Nineteenth-century Jewry, as it emerged from the ghetto into Western culture, properly saw the need for a change in the atmosphere of congregational prayer. Jews could not accept the aesthetic and social conventions of their neighbors in their daily lives without similarly modifying the style and tone of their worship services.

Such cultural adaptation was not new in the history of Jewish prayer. The elegant structures and exalted stance of Spanish Jewish poetry had displaced the intricate wordplay and learned allusions of the original poets of the Holy Land, only in turn to be succeeded in Central and Eastern Europe by a more fervent, free-flowing diction. Now, modern Europe approached things spiritual with dignity, reserve, quiet, and solemnity, and so these qualities, under the heading of " decorum," were transferred to the synagogue. As against its ghetto forebear, today's synagogue displays the sobriety and reserve that are the contemporary conventions of attention. In this tone, the modern Jew recognized cultural clues to what is important and significant. Thus the decorous style of the modern service does indeed prepare him as a citizen of this culture for the worship of God. If personal attention and concentration are crucial to Jewish worship, then surely such an emotional setting will eliminate what modern men consider distracting. This much, and it is important, may be said for the movement to dignify Jewish worship.

After decades of experience, the time has surely come to acknowledge that there has been a loss as well. Insistence on an orderly service has nearly eliminated the active role of the individual worshiper, largely by concentrating the effective conduct of the service in the hands of professional prayer leaders, the rabbi or the cantor. Worshipers are expected to be quiet about their prayer. They must not disturb those around them by raising their voices, crying their grief, or otherwise putting their deeply felt emotion into expression. Rather, they must conform their needs to the congregation's volume, velocity, and emotional level. They are expected to be self-contained — the exact opposite of prayer, which is honest expression from man out to God.

The rabbi and cantor, without anyone's saying a word but with that firmness which culture knows how to impose, are set different limits. They are expected to be more emotional, more personal, as they lead and interpret the prayers. In part, this is because in a group searching for dignity, they can be counted on to do so more effectively. That is to say, the reading of the rabbi and the singing of the cantor will have few, if any, mistakes. They will not hesitate, mispronounce, change keys, lose tone, or become confused. Rather, their renditions can be relied on to be pleasing to the ear, to add beauty to the service. They are aesthetically dependable.

The trained officiant is emotionally dependable as well. True, the range of expression he is permitted is far greater than the congregation's. His knowledge and experience have equipped him not only to show feeling but, more important, never while doing so to transgress the proper social limits. With the worshiper repressed, the beautiful, safe release provided by the rabbi or the cantor now dominates the service.

What began as a necessary, useful alteration of Jewish worship has therefore created its own evils, undermining the very foundations of Jewish prayer. Under the guise of decorum the worshiper has been aesthetically cowed and emotionally neutralized. This is not to say that beautiful music, meaningfully rendered, cannot uplift and exalt the individual congregant. The long tradition of Jewish song and chant, going back farther than that of the prayer texts themselves, speaks eloquently of music's religious value. Likewise, the hoary record of men valued as leaders of congregational prayer, men who for their ability to express their fellows' will in prayer were highly honored, testifies to the virtue of pious and consecrated leadership in worship. The problem is not what good leadership can add, but what it has tended to supplant.

Without individuals investing their thoughts and emotions, their full attention, their devoted selves, in prayer, the Jewish service has lost its meaning. Whenever one listens to the rabbi or cantor, more in peaceful enjoyment than in identification and common meaning, the crucial distinction between the synagogue and the recital hall has been transgressed. Once started on this passive way, the congregation will always find it easier to shift its prayer responsibilities to those whom it has hired to pray for it. They do it so nicely, so dependably. They should really be allowed to do it all — which is but one step from having them do it alone, without benefit of congregants, the congregation thus going from barely participating to not even attending. The rabbi and the cantor must be masters of their craft if they are to lead their congregants, yet they must use their talents to stimulate, not replace, individual participation if they are to keep their services Jewish at their core.

Jewish worship is by belief and practice uncompromisingly individualistic, and its future depends upon the increasing ability of individual Jews to participate in the service and fulfill its expectations.

These general views of prayer in Judaism should not blind us to the fact that the Jewish service is far from a Quaker meeting. Judaism may base its understanding of prayer on the individual man's relation to God, but it refuses to stop there. It does not think of man abstracted from his relation to mankind. It does appreciate the meaning of the individual in isolation, but holds him, the single one, in unremitting importance, against a background of society and history. For the Jew, man is a social and historical creature. Hence, his prayer should properly be a communal, comradely affair. Public worship is a universal human need and, also, a specifically Jewish requirement.

A religion that denied the worth of history might well consider private prayer superior to group prayer. But Judaism's basic view of the universe is historical. The Bible knows man to be almost from his creation a child of history. Man's sin began and still powers the movement of events. But history is no senseless, chance succession. There is a God who rules over time. History has a purpose and a goal — that era when God's rule will be fully established by its manifestation in lives of justice, peace, and love. God's Kingdom-to-be is not a private matter between one individual and God. It must be accomplished with all men and be manifest in all lives, or it is unworthy of the Lord of the universe. The individual man cannot understand himself, cannot properly know his own life's purpose unless he sees it within the context of all mankind and all of history. Isolated from his fellows, he isolates himself from God's social goals.

To want to pray, but only alone and only for oneself, seems therefore to make too much of self, too little of God. Judaism commends communal prayer, because God cares for all as he cares for each one, because, while God is the God of each private individual, he is the God of all individuals as well. The single self is indispensable. Without any one, mankind is incomplete. So, too, without all other selves, equally precious to God, the single self loses its context and hence its final significance. Man cannot find himself only in others, but neither can he find himself without them. If prayer is supposed to open man to the truth of his existence, it must begin with self but it must reach out to all mankind.

Judaism values communal worship, not for its specific Jewish purposes alone, but for all men. Group prayer, by confronting us with others, by asking us to link our prayers to theirs, reminds us immediately and directly that it is never enough to pray for ourselves alone. Speaking as " we," the individual discovers, acknowledges, articulates the needs, desires, hopes, which he though one

man shares with all men because he is not only a private self but
a member of humanity. Besides, when we are conscious of those
with whom we stand, what we may have wanted to pray by ourselves is generally made less selfish, more humble, and therefore
more appropriate for utterance before God. There before us is the
newly bereaved young widower with his three small children.
Near him stand the white-haired man who, close to the age of
retirement, is suddenly faced with bankruptcy; the beautiful young
woman who has just come from the hospital after the removal of
a breast; the quiet mother whose consultation with the school
psychologist was deeply disturbing. When we join *them* in prayer,
when we must, to say, " We," link ourselves with them, we and
our prayer are refined and often exalted far beyond our own means,
for *they are praying now*, lifting us, helping us, with their " we,"
even as they silently reach out to the congregation for compassion
and understanding.

The joy of others similarly affects our worship. We are buoyed
up by the happiness of the new grandparents offering their heartfelt thanks, the engaged couple who will be married this Sunday,
the newly appointed vice-president of his firm, the recently honored community worker. Their joy infuses us so that what might
have been a nagging, niggling, whine of prayer can as a proper
" we " become worthy of God's attention. Indeed, the dynamism,
the momentum, the upreach of a congregation truly at prayer, takes
the individual from the commonplace, the humdrum, the depres-
sion of his daily routine, and projects him and his prayer far beyond himself. The joy of congregational worship is that together,
by a mathematical miracle, individuals transcend the selves they
were before the service began. And prayer does so, not against the
worshiper's intimate individuality, but by calling him, on the most
personal and private level, to do all he can, to lead and lift, to
bear and support, all those with whom he stands.

Social worship is a sharp spur to ethical sensitivity as well as to
enthusiasm. To stand together as equals before God with the man
we dislike, the woman who has cut us, the boors who repel us,
the intellects who snub us, the neighbors we do not trust, the fools

we cannot bear — to say with them in some bond of unity, " we," is to shake our self-righteousness and expand the breadth of our conscience. Much of what we must pray to God is what we share with them in belief, thanksgiving, and petition. And he hears us as one with them. How can we now see them as enemies, adversaries? How can we prevent our prayer from charging us with a new sense of responsibility, not for our immediate synagogue neighbors alone, but for those of our city, our nation, and our world? Here, form and content join in happy harmony. The social context of praying makes immediately practical the ethical imperatives of the prayers themselves. Learning to pray the communal " we " is the first active step in fulfilling every prayer for righteousness and justice. The act of praying together itself commands us; therefore we know it to be commanded.

Nor should these general comments end without a practical word about personal frailty. The individual, when he is his own standard, will pray when he feels he needs to. Prayer, then, finds its occasion and its value in response to his private moods and feelings. What happens under those circumstances to regular prayer with respect to frequency, intensity, and unselfish content is a commonplace of modern versions of religiosity. The man who objects that he cannot pray on schedule often does not pray at all. And when, in this hectic world, he finally allows a conscious desire to pray to take priority over all the important things he should be doing now, he finds he does not have the knack. Obviously prayer in response to the inspiration of a moment has a unique significance, one well worthy of cherishing, but it is a supplement to, not a substitute for, regular public worship — and the acquired habit of turning to God in prayer is readily transferred from the congregational to the private situation.

Where the individual operates by delicious surprise, the community prays by fixed rule. There are two reasons for this. The practical one is: everyone will know when to assemble. The theological one is equally simple. By virtue of devotion to its prophets and saints, the community is less concerned with man's momentary mood than with God's constant presence. If God is real, if he is truly God, men should speak to him, seek him, commune with him regularly — anything less can be considered only folly. And as there is no time when he is not God, when the universe is free of his rule or when men are released from his commandments, so there is no time when men may ignore him with impunity. On God's side, there is no time when prayer is undesirable. Prayer needs to be as regular, as continual, as much a part of living, as is man's continuing dependence on God. Individuals tend to forget or overlook this. Forgetting is their defense against God's ruling their lives. The community has a better memory.

Some religions have pressed this faith to its logical limit and encouraged their adherents to call on God at every moment, generally by ceaselessly repeating his name. Judaism has avoided this rather mechanical, inhuman pattern. God is always ready for prayer, but man is not. Jewish prayer is directed to God but springs from man. Hence, Judaism, in characteristic practical fashion, has sought a rule appropriate to both the partners, one consistent not just with Jewish doctrine but with its goal, to live in history for God's sake. Congregational Jewish services each day are limited to three: morning, afternoon, and evening, with the latter two most often held at twilight and thus combined, as it were, into one service. These regular assemblies remind the Jew, particularly when he attends, but even when he does not, that he should be praying at least twice a day. Is it not true that left to the promptings of his own heart, he will not arrive at even so modest a standard? Modest, that is, if God is God. . . .

Much of the conflict between private and group prayer is really that issue. The synagogue, the congregation of Israel, knows God is real. That knowledge is what created and sustains it. That is why it has prescribed appropriate regularity for its worship. The individual has his doubts and his weaknesses — besides, he is busy. When he believes, and when he remembers, and when he has strength, he will pray. Abraham Heschel's analysis is correct. The problem of prayer is not prayer. The problem of prayer is God. *If* God is real, men should pray — regularly. So says the distant, detached, defensive modern individual. The synagogue says, rather,

The Liturgy and Its Difficulties

since God is real, let us meet to worship him at least twice each day.

Thus, the doctrine of God and man in general that inheres in Jewish faith leads it to command group prayer for religious, ethical, and practical reasons. That is a purely universal judgment, applicable to all men alike. Like much of Judaism's universal content, it is implicit in traditional sources and only rarely explicit. Still, it is part of Judaism and the background which sets off specifically Jewish needs for communal prayer.

The Jew as man, as sharer in the covenant of Noah, is, like all men, enjoined to worship with others. But the Jew shares in the Covenant of Sinai as well — that is what constitutes him a Jew, not just a man — and thus a special necessity for communal prayer acts upon him.

This distinction, being critical to the issue of private versus group prayer in Judaism, demands particular elucidation. To put it bluntly, can Jewishness ever adequately be defined in purely personal terms? (Secular or semisecular but still nontheistic descriptions of the Jews are beyond discussion here. In discussing Jewish worship it is of course the Jew known to the synagogue and prayer book who alone is relevant.) Is being Jewish something that operates privately and so can be expressed in a life of relative isolation? Is Jewish faith only something between each single one and his God alone, so that living one's Judaism does not essentially involve a community?

In part, the answer to these questions must be " Yes." To deny the personal element in the Jew's relationship with God is to deny Judaism's fundamental view of man in general, that he is created in God's image, that he can and should know and serve God. But in larger part, to say that Judaism is merely a religion of individuals requires an emphatic " No." The Judaism of the Bible, the rabbis, the philosophers, the mystics, the Judaism of almost every modern Jewish thinker, and decisively the Judaism of every Jewish prayer book, avers that Judaism is the religion of a people, a folk, a community. " The Jews " are a social entity in their own right, not merely an aggregation of believers. The individual Jew shares in the religion called Judaism as a member of that people-folk-com-munity. His Jewishness, as personally as he may and should feel it, as privately as he may believe and practice it, is not his by virtue of individual discovery or creation, but by his membership in the Household, the Congregation, the Children of Israel. He brings his will, his assent, his reinterpretation to a relationship which God established with this community. He participates in what may, for purposes of corrective exaggeration, be called a group faith, a social religion.

How strange that sounds in a day when men are accustomed to speak of religion as a highly private matter, something each person should decide for himself! This all-pervading personalism (akin to what sociologists have described as " privatism ") stems from several sources. One is surely a reaction to the power of the state. Let it legislate in every area, but let it not require of good and faithful citizens any set religious practice or creed. Another motive derives from a rejection of intolerance and fanaticism. Which religion is truest or what practices within that religion one should follow should ultimately be a matter for each person to decide himself. Compulsion, lay or clerical, being told what one must do by friend or relative, seems an infringement of free-dom and a denial of personal responsibility. For most Americans, the practical content of their religion is consciously regulated by selection and choice. In the end, they follow only their heart or conscience, a standard particularly precious to modern Jews, since it legitimizes their deviation from traditional Jewish law.

Judaism, as the faith of a people, does not deny the individual's right to freedom and judgment. It grants extraordinary liberty to the individual in matters of belief. Today, even in practice, through several organized interpretations of Jewish observance, all of them dynamic, all seeking to make place for personal in-terpretation, the role of the individual has been safeguarded and amplified. The practice and tradition of individuality, one Jew over against other Jews, is legendary.

Nonetheless, religion for the Jew, as the tradition understands it, is not primarily a personal but a communal matter. The Torah was not given to Moses as an individual possession to share with others of a similar mind, but to the Jewish people as a whole. Again and again Moses is commanded, " Speak to the Israelite people and say to them . . ." The Bible is the history of this folk who found God and joined their destiny to him. Its concern with individuals is almost exclusively for those who influenced the life and character of their folk. (The personal side cannot be absent, as the wondrous book of The Psalms, among other examples, makes clear.) The covenant of Noah was made with all mankind, and through it each man has a relation to God. The Covenant at Sinai was made with Israel, the Jewish people, and thus each Jew, as a Jew, shares this unique Jewish relation to God as in inheritor of his people's Covenant.

A religion founded on individual decision might one day find that, through laziness or inattention, few people cared. Where the individual is everything, history and its long-term movement means little or nothing, certainly little more than the history of the individual. Judaism takes the other view. Its God is the righteous Lord of creation who demands and assures that the history he made possible will end in free acceptance of his rule. The sweep is cosmic, the scope all-embracing. Judaism is primarily a religion of history, of God's will for mankind, of human destiny entire, and it envisions Israel's role and the individual's worth against that background. For it remains true, in all the grandeur of this purpose, that there is no history without individuals, no Kingdom of God among men unless he is acknowledged in single souls. Again the individual is indispensable — but against this measure not sufficient or ultimate.

Because its range stretches the limits of finitude, Judaism cannot be satisfied to be a religion whose continuity depends on private human decision. Without an endurance as patient and inexorable as time itself, Judaism's hope to transform and redeem history might be destroyed. As the religion of a people, Judaism counterposes to the individual will to be a Jew social processes whereby the folk itself continues from generation to generation. History and literature, language and land, custom and folkways, all provide historical momentum. Thus too, the Jew enters the Covenant on entering the people by birth, not by decision (though one not born a Jew may, paradoxically enough, take the latter route). One born a Jew may spurn or be indifferent to his people's historic character and toil — but his individual repudiation or indifference cannot change the record of history or the imperatives it creates for those born into the Jewish people. The Covenant of Sinai transcends the individual Jew, as it encompasses him. (The people, too, might as a whole deny its past. Today this is not hypothetical speculation. But Jewish faith includes faith in Israel as it is based on faith in God.)

Judaism is a folk religion because this best suits its religious goals. Jewish peoplehood is an indispensable part of Jewish religious thought and Jewish religious practice. A specifically Jewish religious life, as contrasted to that of Noahide man in general, means, therefore, life in and with the Jewish people, the Covenant community.

Jewish worship is, classically, communal in character. Its Jewishness derives not from the external facts that Hebrew is used, traditional texts are recited, or Jewish symbols are displayed. It is Jewish because it is born out of the Covenant at Sinai and articulates Israel's bond with its God. The special language, texts, and symbols all stem from this root relationship. Jewish worship, then, is the people of Israel, assembled before its God out of continuing loyalty to their Covenant, to acknowledge, praise, and petition him. The group may be small; traditionally as few as ten are acceptable for a full public service. When at least ten Jews congregate to pray, they constitute the Covenant folk in miniature. They represent all Israel, past and present, here and everywhere. Not ten or more individuals, but the Covenant people itself now confronts its God. The man who prays in the synagogue prays as a participant in a Jewish history that continues into the living present, and his prayers, therefore, express the needs of the community in which he stands. Jewish law is clear. The individual Jew should seek to pray with a congregation. But if he cannot (that great phrase without which nothing could endure in history), then he may pray alone. Even alone, he should pray the congregational service (with some deletions), preferably at the time the congregation is praying. For a Jew, one's individuality is connected with being one (*sic!*) of the Jewish people, sharer in mutual Covenant with God.

The Jewish prayer book, the *siddur*, speaks out of this particular situation of the people of Israel gathered yet again to meet its God, to renew their ancient pact and beseech his current help. That is why most of its prayers are in the plural. They speak of " us," of " our," of " we." This plural should be taken with full seriousness, in all its useful ambiguity. " We " may only mean " I," put in a rather formal, or editorial plural — important, since without " me " there is no meaningful prayer. " We " may mean " this group with whom I am now praying" and therefore myself and my neighbors. It surely also means " this congregation or community," those who should be here but may not be, those with whom we share our Jewish hopes, labors, and anxieties. It means all of these — but including these, and embracing them, it means primarily "We, the people of Israel, the folk of the Covenant." Now what might have been a tiny, almost selfish "we " has risen from our cosy group in its familiar associations to embrace all of history in loyalty and obedience to its Master. Through this great Jewish " we " the individual " I " has found an incomparable dignity and an immeasurable worth. This is the boon which worship as a member of the Covenant people freely bestows.

This is also the source of the special problem of Jewish prayer today. With some good fortune, modern man may be able to admit that he has faith, that he believes in God. He may even be able to overcome his embarrassment enough to learn to pray to him. But this is personal religion, *his* God, met on *his* terms and in response to *his* needs. These prayers are intimate indeed, else they could not arise. The *siddur* asks him to pray to Israel's God of the Covenant — and to make Israel's Covenant-based prayers his prayers. What a gap to bridge, what a chasm to cross! If the problem of prayer in general is God, then the problem of

Jewish prayer is *Israel.* To pray as one of this historic people, identifying oneself with its membership and its mission, that is the demand made of modern Jewish man by the *siddur.*

Contrast this challenge with the tone of much else of today's society. Modern America is unthinkable without the thorough-going commitment to please the consumer and satisfy his individual needs. Banks say they will be his friend; automobile companies seek to give him status; cigarette makers almost openly promise to enhance his sexuality; politicians mold themselves to the image he desires. Millions of dollars and countless hours of creative research are expended each year in an effort to lay bare the individual's current dissatisfactions, to reach him on a level he can enjoy, and to fulfill his remaining unfulfillments. Moreover, many now promise him that there are no risks involved; no charge will be made until he has received the first gratifications, or if not satisfied, he may have his money back or even double. Modern man is trained to the consumer role. He waits patiently, even in boredom. The seller must please him — or else.

Many a religious institution has sought to meet modern man on this level, to sell its wares, to appeal to the religious market in terms of the benefits its services provide. Attending group worship keeps families together, soothes housewives' nerves, and decreases managerial ulcers or coronaries. Religion permeates deeper, affects distressed areas speedier, brings longer lasting comfort.

These claims are not unwarranted. Religion can and has changed men's lives for the good, and what it offers is so poorly known that it needs the techniques of public relations to reach the unaffiliated. That is not the issue here. When a religious institution renounces its knowledge and tradition of the holy as its basic criterion of activity, particularly its worship, when consciously or unconsciously its new goal is the American pattern of pleasing the consumer, it has begun its own self-destruction. It has made the congregant/consumer, not God, the focus of its concern — and although the service of God does not require ignoring man's desires, it is clear where the real priorities lie. The worship of the synagogue and the content of the prayer book reflect God's preeminence and see the needs of the individual fused with those of his religious community, the Jewish people.

The gap between Jewish prayer and American consumer logic as it applies to religion can be clarified by noting its effects. A man finally decides to come to a service. He has been told for so long that it will be good for him that he decides to give it a try. He waits for something to happen. Perhaps the music soothes him a little, the quiet is assuaging, the prayers are comforting, and the sermon is not only understandable but even somewhat inspiring. Some consumers are satisfied with such rewards. Most are not, which is why attendance at worship is poor. They frankly find more than an occasional visit, for reasons of sociability or habit, unsatisfying. As they say, they don't "feel anything special." Nothing unique "happens" to them that cannot be duplicated in more palpable or less demanding form. Religion really does not "do anything" for them. It doesn't "produce" when given a try.

From this general experience, consumer logic inevitably concludes: the fault is with the institution, in this case the synagogue, and its prayer book in particular. To get people to services today, the deduction follows, they must have a religion that fits in with their immediate way of life. Thus it is foolish to use a prayer book written centuries ago, in a remote poetic style, about vague generalities that largely fail to express contemporary experience. A few of the old prayers or practices should be retained for emotional or symbolic reasons (the new modernity knows that emotions are important), but the only successful service today would be one that embodied and articulated the very present needs of those praying.

This suggestion runs into great difficulty whenever men seek to put it into practice. Most free and unregimented liturgies (Methodist, Baptist — even the patterns of Quaker meetings or Jewish youths' "creative" services), when they continue from week to week and month to month, fall into a standard format and a regular style. Spontaneity is not easily regularized. Moreover, the personal needs of the congregants are not easy to discover in depth nor to express in a fresh and appealing way. As a result, attempts at a personalized service generally end up a mixture of the customary and the creative, with both the traditionalists and the individualists unhappy with the results.

Why not, however, utilize modern technology to follow this theory to its logical conclusion? No rabbi or committee, regardless of assistance or library resources, could be as effective in identifying the inner needs of worshipers at one given moment and creating a service from modern and ancient materials, verbal and musical, to express them, as a properly stocked and programmed computer. The possibilities both in diagnosing needs and responding to them in varied format are exhilarating. A checklist of moods and emotions could be provided for each prospective worshiper to determine his individual situation, or if that is too superficial, some sort of religious inkblots that would allow him to project his depth desires. Each Friday before sundown, the worshiper would phone the computer, and according to a prearranged code, feed it his need data as of the present moment. Thus he would know that Friday evening's service would reflect his personal situation, and having also participated in its creation, he would be very likely to attend. On its part, the computer would be a model of rabbinic openness, gratefully and patiently accepting all calls with understanding — perhaps, by simple wiring modifications, even several at one time!

The creation of such a service would be speedy but to the highest standards. Experts in religious worship would previously have programmed the machine with the most varied possible patterns of effective religious services, as well as having provided a feedback device that limited the frequency of their repetition. At a given time before the service, to keep the need data as current as possible, the computer would devise the evening's service. First, it would mathematically determine the exact proportion of moods which would be present. Then from the entire range of literature in its memory section, perhaps worldwide as well as Jewish, it would draw selections appropriate to the needs. These, according to a pattern effective for the night's goal, would be struc-

tured into a service. The next chore would be typing and du-
plicating (printing, in more affluent congregations), the computer
efficiently making only as many copies as there would have been
calls, plus extras based on experience at this time of the year,
with this weather, with such and such competitive activities
going on, as to how many others would come. A truly sophisticated installation would provide for evaluation, registering the
congregation's response to this service and including such responses
as part of its guidance for the future. Thus, so to speak, the computer could learn to *create* even more effective services.

One more of the many other values of this system must be
mentioned: help with preaching. Surely the sermon, too, should
speak to authentic congregational situations. Hence the computer
might guide the preacher in his choice of text or approach. Better yet, the energetic preacher would stock his computer with
a variety of sermons (again based on the computer's memory and
analysis of previous congregational need patterns and reactions),
and the computer, while selecting materials for a particular
service, could also select the sermon most appropriate to it. What
is more, the electronic brain could be relied upon to keep the
manuscript, if not the delivery, down to a length carefully ad-
justed to the congregation's, not the preacher's, needs.

What is satire here will one day be attempted in all seriousness. Those who are committed to the religion of individual needs
should obviously do what they can to make their faith function
better.

Judaism has traditionally sought the standard of its practice
and the chief guide of its observance in another direction. What
it cannot do, what it believes no religion can hope to do and
still be worthy of ultimate concern, is to make the individual worshiper the final measure of the value of the synagogue in general or the Jewish service in particular. When every judgment is
based on whether the prayer book moves him personally, whether
the ceremonies satisfy his intimate longings, the question must
inevitably also arise whether God also adequately serves him.
Now, the essential blasphemy of this position becomes clear.

When religion abandons itself to consumers and makes them its judge, it has created a new and false god in place of the one and only God. This false and fickle god of the public will betray its "religious" leaders and institutions today as in its various guises it has in the past.

This does not mean that religion cannot in part be evaluated by how it responds to the human situation, nor does this mean to deny that every religion must in significant part meet man on his own level. The sin lies in making this the exclusive or even dominant goal. Man does have needs but, if one may dare to say it, so does God — rather, man's needs are best met in terms of God's will, his law, his purposes. Religion is more God's commands than man's desires, God's goals than man's dreams, God's presence than man's existence, though both are critical. Man fulfills himself in serving God, not in pursuit of anything he ever was or in his imperfection might, without God, imagine himself to be. That is what Jewish tradition implicitly understood as it sought to relate each man through the community and its discipline to God, and thus to his fullest self. The synagogue and its communal worship are built on that premise. If the modern Jew is to learn to pray as a Jew, and not just as man in general, he does not need a better prayer book but a better theology, not a different form of worship but a deeper belief.

Or perhaps he needs to be helped to realize what in the depths of his soul he somehow still does believe, that he is both individual *and* Jew, single one *and* member of the Covenant folk. Then perhaps he can reach beyond the shallow self-centeredness that characterizes so much of modern man's life and is responsible for its pervasive subsurface anxiety, and learn to say ever more wholeheartedly the "we" that must always begin with and lead back to the self, the "we" that reaches out beyond the individual, beyond neighbors, beyond the congregation, to embrace all the people of Israel (and through the people of Israel, all mankind), and to affirm with such a "we" this one Jew's place among his people before its God. Then, in sum, he will pray *as a Jew*, and praying as a Jew will know what his life of prayer can mean to him as a private self.

It is a paradoxical faith that produces the pattern and structures of Jewish worship. Each individual can and should pray for himself — but a Jew prays as one of the Covenant people. Jewish prayer is simultaneously individual and communal, and the *siddur* is Judaism's living response to the demands of this faith.

PART III

SPEAKING TO THE CULTURAL CONTEXT

Chapter

8

THE VARIETIES OF APOLOGETIC STRATEGY

Judaism still has much to say to its children whose intellect is
largely nourished by secular culture — so runs the positive refrain
of the continuing lament that they disdain their heritage. That
apologetic confidence was put to the test when *Commentary*
magazine invited fifty Jewish thinkers to answer five questions on
Judaism which it felt concerned its readers. Thirty-eight replies
were received and have been published as a book entitled *The
Condition of Jewish Belief*. Considering the rather negative, even
snide attitudes most Jewish community leaders have toward the
magazine, only its unique audience explains the breadth of the
participation. For the *Commentary* subscriber is the Jewish intellectual par excellence. He is, according to a recent article on
the American intellectual establishment, really the general American intellectual — which says a great deal about the interplay between Jewishness and urban intellectuality in the United States
today! The symposium, then, was that rare opportunity for those
who stand within the circle of Jewish commitment to speak to
those Jewish secular intellectuals who stand at various points
near its circumference.

That is the classic situation for apologetic theology, the believer invited to explain his faith to the serious inquirer. With so
many respondents coming from so broad a range of institutional

and personal backgrounds it should be possible to derive a good idea of the alternative structures being employed for apologetic theology today.

The most striking thing about the contributions, as the introduction notes, is the essential irrelevance of the Jewish denominational lines. Leave out the labels with which some authors tag themselves or their identifications and it becomes quite difficult to tell the Reform Jews from the Conservative and, for the greater part of their response, the Orthodox from either of the two.

The critical division among the authors seems to be found more in terms of age than of institutions. A line, set roughly at about fifty, marks off, with some exceptions, two substantially different approaches to explaining Judaism. If one reads the older men, then regardless of their affiliation, the tone of the response is remarkably consistent. Their most obvious joint characteristic is their need to identify themselves institutionally, as if this, contrary to what the rest of the symposium indicates, establishes some specific religious content. They are also at pains to show that they have a modern, enlightened attitude toward the Jewish past and they regularly glorify and justify it in terms of ethical idealism. They vary somewhat as to the place of peoplehood in Judaism but they all affirm its significance and always in terms of a more significant and embracing universalism. They do not speak as much of God as about man, and where they do, he tends to be somewhat abstract and distant, as befits a force or an idea.

No one can say that the approach of these sages will not in the long run be the most appealing to Jewish intellectuals, yet that is difficult to believe on the basis of past performance and present predilection. This cultured, dignified Judaism has held the center of the stage among Jews for over thirty years now with only minor modifications, with modest results as far as Jewish intellectuals were concerned. On that count alone a change of tactics would seem desirable. Moreover, when one compares this sort of appeal with the argumentation current today among intellectuals generally, the disparity is vast. The reader being addressed has a broad-ranging cultural interest founded on substantial information. He is sophisticated, which means that he does not want a rehash of old ideas but the pioneer concepts in the field involved, if not with the immediacy of an academic journal, then only one step below. He is already highly ethically motivated, as he thinks, without a specially Jewish foundation, and his commitments run so deep that he insists that every discussion of economics or city planning, and certainly of politics, must ultimately consider the ethical goals of human existence. Yet he is an insistent realist, concerned with power interests in society and ego-sexual drives among individuals. He is a critical intelligence, refusing to accept the answers old or new without the most unsparing probing. His ritual slaughter is of sacred cows. He is increasingly nonideological and suspicious of institutions. He is, at its best, the secular mind of much "death of God" theology.

The problem of communication between him and the older symposiasts comes out clearly in the matter of literary style. The senior generation will sometimes call on sentiment or rhetoric to move from secular reason to religious affirmation. That is, to the intellectual, the unforgivable sin in argument. Nothing is as critical to him as the struggle to be free of illusion and thereby make possible some genuine integrity. The younger apologetes may talk of mystery, but they do not rhapsodize about it, nor do they leave it without questioning and rational checks and balances.

The younger men seem to speak in more familiar intellectual tones, though they occasionally employ an unfamiliar jargon that comes naturally with their expertise. Thus, they are highly nonideological in theory and deeply personally involved in what they say. They seem more in the midst of thinking than arrived at solutions. They are open to diverse influences yet insist on basic commitments. Their style tends to be lean, and their concern for the ultimate issues taken in a fully serious way. They are still somewhat self-conscious about this sort of writing and an occasional pulpit flourish occasionally obtrudes. Still, their questioning personalism is a long way from the dignified self-assurance of their seniors.

Substantively, what divides the generations is revelation. It is the key concept among all the younger men, and, though they may differ as to its extent, they know it is not simply human discovery. For God is a real and present reality to them and not just a concept. Their sense of Jewishness comes from living under his commandments in the here and now. These they know from tradition and from their personal experience of God's commanding presence. They are, in various ways, religious existentialists, substituting the new language of person and relationship for the older philosophic languages of ideas, experiences, or social values.

This approach is so pervasive that the introduction complains slightly at the sameness of the statements. One does miss a new and different intellectual ground in this group. Among Protestants the Whiteheadians appear and the influence of linguistic analysis occasionally emerges. Among Roman Catholics, Teilhard de Chardin creates excitement, but the Jewish rationalists have in recent years been submitting few informed new statements to the criticism of learned colleagues. Perhaps this absence is what the concluding call of the introduction for more theological discussion in the Jewish community meant.

This fundamentally existentialist position cannot, however, be attributed to the influence of Franz Rosenzweig to the detriment of Martin Buber's role. Without the former, it is true, the modern discussion would be without two of its most precious formulations: that revelation can be real even if the texts which state it are shaped by men, and that the man who accepts his Jewish identity should accept the Law in principle if not yet in all its traditional working out. Nonetheless, without Buber it would not be possible for modern men to rely on Rosenzweig, for they cannot follow Rosenzweig's path to Jewish commitment. He found his way through the rejection of the German idealistic philosophy and then by a sudden, unexplained move into the Jewish faith. American Jews do not start in idealism, so they cannot go even the negative way with him; and since it is not clear why he took on the faith he did, he is of little help to those who stand confused along the way, though they know he finally stands where they would like to be.

That is precisely where Buber helps. He has made as clear as one is likely to be able to do the source of belief and the reason for its open, personalist texture today. Because Buber's image of the I-Thou has been accepted by many thinkers in the modern world, the modern Jew can speak of faith and even revelation with substantial integrity. Moreover, Buber clarifies the particular Jewishness of the basic commitment. Rosenzweig, in those writings of the post World War I era, seems little more than a racialist in his corporate discussions, as Buber himself of that day now seems to read. Buber managed to live and think on to the critical concept that eliminates blood from the question of Jewish uniqueness yet did not lose ethnicity in universality. Buber created the modern meaning of Covenant, the relationship between the people of Israel and its God, the unique social parallel to what takes place between individuals and God. "Covenant" is not Rosenzweig's usual term or concept. Yet if the Covenant is real, then against Buber and with Rosenzweig the modern Jew knows why there is law, for relationship imposes duty, as Buber has taught, and communal duty means law. Without Buber's careful thought the thinking Jew could not use Rosenzweig's institutions.

Finally, on the issue of the truth of Christianity, the contributors reject Rosenzweig's full equality of truth for Buber's more cautious judgment of its different and, to a Jew, less appealing truthfulness. So Buber is the hidden hero of the symposium, though it is doubtful he will ever get the credit. There seems to be a compulsion, particularly noticeable among Conservative rabbis who are eager to justify Law, though with changes, to denigrate Buber. This says less about their actual reliance upon him than it does about their fear that if one follows his rationale of Jewish faith, one might as easily accept his freedom to the tradition as wind up in Rosenzweig's loyalty.

The bulk of the symposium, then, elaborates the varieties of

existentialist Jewish apologetic. Seven distinctive points along the
spectrum of opinion may be located.

The first illustrates well the basic frustration of communication engendered by the personalist basis of existentialist commitment. The thinker knows the truth of his position from the way
it functions in his life, including his rationality. Yet since life
is bigger than concepts can ever be, he cannot hope to give convincing reasons for his faith. Hence he limits himself to the subjective adequacy of his position. The difficulty with such personalism is that in the effort not to make universal cognitive
claims for one's statement, one leaves the reader feeling that a
psychological rather than a theological document has been read
and thus one that does require his assent.

This understanding, that the author's truth is essentially personal, becomes more appealing when it shows what being a Jew
means in one man's life in a way that the reader knows is parallel
to his own. The hope here is that what cannot be conveyed by
idea will be conveyed in terms of personal reality, as in the famous response of a Hasid who, when asked why he went to see
his *rebbe*, said that it was to see him tie his shoe. As some of the
authors arrange their laces, one cannot help being moved.

Yet personal example must lead the individual to more cognitive concerns. That is why most of the men in this group,
though conceding that all faiths are ultimately beyond explanation, do what they can to show Judaism's reasonableness. One
author is quite careful to indicate what he considers to be not
only the Jewish grounds for rejecting Communism and Fascism
while requiring social reconstruction, yet he does not hesitate to
indicate that he sees Jewish limits as to what the underprivileged
may claim from the majority. Another contributes something of
a tour de force in deriving the entire content of Jewish Law from
the commandments to love God and fellowman. Perhaps that is
why he is one of the few authors who follow Rosenzweig in accepting Christianity as fully true. A third carefully shows how Jewish scholarship as well as Jewish commitment makes it impossible

for the concept of the chosen people to be considered a doctrine of racial superiority or special privilege.

Yet it is only in the case of Emil Fackenheim that one has the feeling that although faith may be subjective, it is in such intimate tension with rigorous intellectuality that the two have become one. There is almost nothing in his response which does not explain or reason with the reader. He begins his discussion of revelation with an existentialist understanding of the necessity of particularity (of ideas necessarily having reality only in relation to specific situations and persons) and carefully rejects all gross universalizing and self-justifying abstractions as a less true and less significant level of religious understanding than Biblical and contemporary particularism. He can then move carefully from question to question to show why this fundamental insight can clarify and even commend a reasonably traditional Jewish faith.

There remain, however, limits to what Fackenheim's patient rationality can accomplish. Though he makes the content of his Jewish faith sound more rationally acceptable than anyone else, what chance is there the reader will let himself be convinced? Do not the very questions posed before the symposiasts indicate the inquirer's commitment to skepticism? Thus five or six respondents felt compelled to point out that the request to Hillel to learn the whole Torah on one foot came from a pagan. A Jew would know better. If the questioner is not simply open but negative, neither reasonableness nor rationality will do. Every Jew who has had the experience of jousting with intellectuals knows that most of them do not want to discuss, much less learn. They want to justify their nonobservance. Perhaps, then, the best thing to do is not to try to justify Judaism at all, but simply state its truth and let the intellectuals do what they want with it. That dogmatic approach is taken by both Arthur Hertzberg and Arnold Wolf. The former knows that after all the appeal of monotheism and the beauty of ethics it is only the affirmation of chosenness which will make a man opt for the burdens of Jewish existence. The other destroys every question put to him by indicating why from the standpoint of an overpowering sense of God's presence, the questions, seemingly so enlightened, are not just wrong but dangerous.

Yet the strategic retreat within can be matched by the radical stride without. Both Zalman Schachter and Richard Rubenstein seem bent on showing that they can be more secular, more modern, more nonconformist than their supposedly tuned-in reader. Judaism need not be squarely bourgeois, for it is really the revolution beyond all other revolutions. For Schachter that not only means that Buddhism and Judaism are finally one, but that any means of attaining this transcendent sense of unity, including drugs, must be considered legitimate. Rubenstein's radicalism is comparatively staid, resting as it does on the death of God with a concomitant attempt to justify religious practice on the grounds of psychoanalytic need.

The latter two positions have gone so far to try to appeal to the outsider that one might reasonably inquire whether they have not begun to step beyond the bounds of Judaism. Yet that is the root problem of almost all the approaches. By agreeing to speak to the intellectual in his own terms, by accepting his secular frame of reference as the criterion of meaning, the writers have subjected themselves to impossible cognitive burdens and, what is worse, implicitly acknowledged the superior position of secularism and its right to judge religion. Only Hertzberg and Wolf refuse to knuckle under to this external, constricted sense of what is real and valuable in the universe. They will not play the secularist's game. They prefer to stand up in all dignity and say the religious truth as they see it rather than to risk demeaning their Judaism in the effort to make it secularly agreeable.

Yet there is a further option that the existentialist analysis of the nature of faith holds open. It is to recognize that even the supposedly unbelieving inquirer founds his life on faith. If he asks his question out of a deep, existential seriousness, then he is asking out of his own commitments or his faith. Insofar as his questions are real they do not come out of a theoretical free-floating, detached philosophic mind, but out of a particular man with his specific beliefs. Whether he or we recognize it or not, he asks out of his faith, his secular faith, and the difficulty in speaking to him rationally is that faith is resisting faith, not inquiring of reason. Until he realizes what he is doing, reason will be his rationalization for resisting Judaism and remaining with his unconscious but real religion.

That is why, in my own contribution to the symposium, I felt that there must be a polemic part to this apologetic discussion. One must bring the inquirer to see that this dialogue is not between his enlightened, impartial reason and subjective mystic Judaism, but between two types of faith, one as personal as the other. The ultimate issue is not whether Judaism can be demonstrated to be as rational as enlightened secularism, but only which faith is more adequate to the human situation in its radical depth. That challenge to his faith before presenting Judaism not only preserves the latter's dignity, but finally gives it a chance properly to commend itself. For now the discussion is between equals, and the value of secularism is as much in doubt and as much required to substantiate itself as is Judaism.

More, it frequently turns out with secularized Jews that their faith is not simply what any intelligent man of our time will hold and what the general tendency of our culture is. The more realistic and hardheaded the intellectual is, the more he should see that Western culture is not easily described as ethical. Its secular institutions do not create sacrificially ethical masses, nor does its philosophy or intellectual mood inculcate a strong sense of ethical responsibility. The man who is passionately devoted to ethical goals, whose concern for the ethical is, in fact, his substitute for religion, may then be asked how he substantiates this for himself to the point of lifelong devotion and how he proposes that it survive with historical effectiveness to transform history. This line of questioning arises from the belief that this urban intellectual ethicism is fundamentally set upon the remnants of Judaism, its law and its messianism. Jewish faith has been secularized into intense human concern. If so, the intellectual's faith remains, at root, Jewish faith, only now it has become a shallow surface thing. Expose its missing depth and there is a chance that its continuing relation to the Jewish God and the experience of the Jewish people may be seen. What started, then, as apparently outside, abstract questions have now been shown, in terms of the commitments of the questioner, to be shared Jewish concerns, and there is a possibility that he may come to accept himself as one who shares a fuller Jewish faith. That is the somewhat optimistic aspiration of polemical apologetics represented in the symposium by my own contribution.

Yet now that the essays have been published and the world has had the opportunity of being exposed to " the best minds of modern Judaism," nothing seems to have changed at all. Judaism still does not get equal time with music, art, plays, books, and politics. The symposium attracted almost no press comment except in the Yiddish dailies, the *Forverts* and *Der Tog*, and drew only about a dozen letters to the editor, some nasty, most simply unfavorable. The temptation is to blame the editors. Had they wanted to have some controversy, the editors should have, in advance of publication, sent out the galley proofs to distinguished personages, requesting comment, as they often do.

These are as trivial complaints from the Jewish side as the boredom of the contributions is from the intellectuals' side. Rereading today the famous symposium of the young intellectuals in the April, 1961, issue of *Commentary*, one is reminded of how tedious *those* thirty-some respondents were then, though one kept reading out of a gossipy concern to know what the next new culture hero would say, and out of a masochistic compulsion to see what the next Jewish atrocity would be. The present symposium contains no "great" names, at least not in the universe of the secular intellectual. Worse, it contains no sensations. These men affirm Judaism. They believe in God, his Covenant with Israel, and the responsibility to live under the Law which flows from it. That isn't news, just Judaism; and the intellectual doesn't want to take it seriously lest he have to change his way of life. When Commentary becomes the substitute for Text, one can hardly expect the old truths, even in new dress, to have much effect.

Believing Jews delude themselves when they trust that this or that style of explanation, or some new one being elaborated in the as yet unrecognized philosophy of some obscure genius, will reclaim the intellectuals. The entire community, nuclear as well as marginal, is shaped by deep-running social forces, reinforced by tenacious psychoanalytic dynamisms, and no apologetic stance will charm the peripheral from their position and draw them to the center. That may be distressing, as is the sinfulness of every Jew, beginning with the believers, but it should not engender despair. Nor should the intellectuals' continuing distance, nor the difficulty of reaching them, so clearly elucidated by this symposium, relieve the community of the need to try to communicate with them. They are brothers in a family that cherishes every soul. They are intelligent people, and Judaism values highly those who are learned. From time to time, it may be possible to convince a few, or better, provide the context in which their desire to reclaim their Jewish roots may take effect. The day may come when there are many more. Until then theologians must persevere in their work because they believe the day will come when all men, including secular intellectuals, will come to learn Torah, if not from his limited apologists, then plainly from God himself.

Chapter
9

A SOFT WORD TO WRITERS

The relationship between the American Jewish community and its estranged or semiestranged intellectual children would provide excellent material for high comedy, not the least because it has such serious overtones. The community bursts with pride when the young succeed, and it cannot contain its curiosity about their attitude to Judaism or affiliation, only to become depressed regularly when the young seem to have a sense of having outgrown "that sort of thing." The occasional discussions between them and the community sound for all the world as if " the Jews " are justifying their own youthful rejection of the seductions of flight, while the marginal men are proving once and for all why they were right in not becoming rabbis. Perhaps one day a gifted *farceur* will make it possible for them to talk to one another decently by teaching them how to laugh a little at their mutual fears and pretensions.

The straight-faced effort might better be served today by a change of method. Instead of opening up the usual exchange of negations, why not see what possibilities arise from a comparison of affirmations? Some books by Jews who are renowned literary critics and several articles by well-known novelists will serve as a good basis for a sample inquiry.

On the whole, the literary people would seem the most difficult group of intellectuals to reach because secular culture, at its best, claims to give them a satisfactory substitute, perhaps a fulfillment of the values of Judaism. As a "second civilization," as a source of cultural enrichment — literature, art, and music — Judaism cannot have great appeal to them. Its aesthetic excellence is modest, and the competition of world culture is too keen. East European Jewish culture provides a fair test, since it was a mature development as contrasted with the youth and rawness of the American and Israeli varieties today. As literature the beloved Yiddish stories must be judged second-rate. That was the verdict of Irving Howe and Eliezer Greenberg in their masterful introduction to their collection, A Treasury of Yiddish Stories.[1] Norman Podhoretz, in his long, largely autobiographical review essay, said of this literature simply, "Very little of this has anything to do with that part of me which reads English."[2] If Jewish culture demands special effort, why should this not be expended on other auxiliary cultures, such as those of Africa or Southeast Asia, which are almost totally unknown but have an increasing impact on American lives? So many possibilities of cultural enrichment keep becoming available these days that the real problem is which ones not to reject. If the argument shifts from intrinsic cultural worth to nostalgia, that is an appeal to forgo intellectual freedom, and as such must be spurned.

If Judaism has anything to offer a modern, cultured man, it is a faith by which to power and guide living. Its distinctive accent is more metaphysical than aesthetic. Dialogue with Jewish intellectuals must inevitably turn on theological issues.

Surprisingly enough, if one may accept their occasional affirmations, the literary intellectuals are agreed as to the importance of basing life on faith. Their careers are one continuous act of spiritual commitment, as they explicitly acknowledge. Introducing his book, The Promised End, Stanley Edgar Hyman says: "The essays have a few themes that never disappear," of which one is "literature as secular salvation and redemption."[3] Alfred Kazin declares:

In many American colleges and universities just now we
have virtually no other way of approaching fundamental
questions except through the materials furnished by contemporary literature. And it has been my experience that
the critic who teaches literature is now the focus for values
and influence that in other cultures are furnished by the
family, religion, political ideologies.[4]

The very style of literary criticism, he acknowledged, reflects this.
The critic "writes dramatically, marshaling his evidence in a
way that pure logic would never approve and pure scholarship
would never understand, but which is justifiable, if it succeeds,
as moral argument in the great tradition of literature." [5]

For the critics, the devotion to literature requires a continuing
act of faith, because the empirical evidence, the reality of literature, does not justify it. So much is so bad, and the situation
seems to be getting increasingly worse. In an early essay Hyman
had found some good in the modern novel, but concluded: "We
can do no more than hope for its consummation [as a major art of
the novel] in our time." [6] On including this essay in *The Promised End*, he felt compelled to add: "Since writing [this] . . .
I have discovered that things are much worse than I thought, and
that the flood of trash is exceeded only by the flood of puffery
expended on it by well-known writers and critics." [7] His devotion
to literature is, like the halachah, less a self-commending pleasure
than a purifying discipline. He says: "Genuine art is demanding
and difficult, often unpleasant, nagging at the mind and stretching the nerves taut." [8] Kazin puts the *Akedah*, the Isaac-binding
of the literary believer, this way:

> While I see a host of brilliantly talented writers all around
> me, I don't often get a very profound satisfaction out of
> the novels they write. I am tired of reading for compassion
> instead of pleasure. . . . The heart of my complaint [is]
> . . . the dimness, the shadowiness, the flatness, the paltri-
> ness in so many reputable novelists.[9]

Yet, he says, "whatever my complaints, I never despair of the novel." [10] The same "despite it all" applies to criticism as well:

> One of the things that we don't talk about, that some of us never even notice, is the absence of echo to our work, the uncertainty of response, the confusion of basic terms in which we deal. . . . Literature no longer seems to exercise much influence.[11]

Irving Howe's blistering denunciation of what has happened to literature and publishing since World War II is one of the most telling parts of his famous essay, "This Age of Conformity." [12] The words, the tone, sound as if they were borrowed from discussions of the future of Judaism.

Podhoretz' more cautious position may be in part a reaction to the tradition of literature for literature's sake which he saw rigidly exemplified at Cambridge. For him, literature must serve life. So his attitude toward it is "agnostic rather than religious: I do not go to literature for the salvation of my soul, but only to enlarge or refine my understanding, and I do not expect it to redeem the age, but only to help the age become less chaotic and confused." [13] Yet contrast this detachment with the characteristic passion and intensity of his articles. In an age of cool observers who prefer stylistic competence to the risk of taking a stand, Podhoretz stands out precisely because he is fully engaged with his subject. Nothing less than an ultimate concern for what writing can mean for life will explain the distinctive tone of his essays. Moreover, he, too, knows that most literature does not deserve this flaming commitment. "Only a very small fraction of the books published every year in this country are worth the typewriter ribbons they have worn through." [14] Nor does the response to his own work explain it.

> Everyone who writes . . . is often afflicted with the feeling that all he is doing is dropping stone after stone down the bottomless well of American culture. Who listens? Who

cares? What difference does any of it make? There is no
easy answer to questions like these, and in the end we are
all thrown back, if we are lucky, upon a simple animal
faith.[15]

The literary critic must live by his faith. Although faith is no
substitute for intelligence, taste, and skill, it is the manifest
presence of their faith which gives the work of these men its special power and significance. So it should be possible to speak with
them of the place of faith in life, and of the more important
question: What is an adequate faith?

The problem of theodicy does not seem to be a firm barrier
to discussion with these intellectuals, unexpected as that might
seem. In their own way, each has found the courage to affirm faith
in the goodness of existence and the continuing significance of
moral action. Although rejecting doctrinaire solutions to contemporary social problems, Howe is still able to believe enough
in man, in human reason, and in their potential in this universe,
to remain a dedicated socialist in politics. This primacy of the
moral to the human permeates his criticism. He detects a moral
commitment in the poet Wallace Stevens and is at pains to identify Sholom Aleichem as less a "folksy humorist" than one
notable for his "moral poise and his invulnerability to ideological
fashions." [16] He is outraged at Norman Mailer's praise (in *The
White Negro*) for the courage of two young punks who express
their primal violence, though the result was that they beat an
old storekeeper to death. A similar insistence on the "moral imagination" runs through much of Hyman's criticism, and he insists
that there cannot be any good literature without it.[17]

Kazin expands this affirmation to embrace the goodness of life
itself.

One of the things we now long for in contemporary literature is escape from the tyranny of symbolic "meaning." We
want to return to life not as a figure in the carpet but as life
in its beautiful and inexpressible materiality — life as the

gift that it actually is rather than as the "material" that
we try to remake.[18]

Thus he criticizes Malamud for too much symbolism; Roth for
too much design; Robert Penn Warren for theorizing; Algren for
lack of compassion; Durrell for improperly mixing imagination
and reality; Capote for rejecting actual human relationships.[19]
Podhoretz is far more positive. He criticizes Dwight MacDon-
ald's acceptance of a high culture for intellectuals and a middle-
brow culture for the mass, because of the negativism toward man
implicit in such a stand, and he commends the active social
imagination of writers like Paul Goodman who show the continuing relevance of man's faith in his capacities. He derides the Beat
writers for their poverty of feeling and technique, and equally for
their love of brutality as against morality and intellectuality. He
faults Roth for his negativism (in *Letting Go*) but is unhappy
with the private, almost mystic affirmation of life in Bellow, Gold,
and Styron, concluding with his own credo:

> But if . . . the malaise, the sense of purposelessness, the
> apathy, the boredom, the difficulty of communication be-
> tween persons — are in fact the products not of Fate or of
> Life or of Being, but of a particular form of economic or-
> ganization and a particular set of political arrangements,
> then to accept them as inexorable is to brand oneself a
> coward or a fool.[20]

These men may not have a theory of suffering, but they have
enough faith to live with it and give their lives to moral striving.
This does not sound so distant from the normative Jewish position that it should make discussion futile. Again, what should
make the exchange of interest is how deep such a faith must go.
Having read this much into the affirmations of these critics, it
will not do to suggest that they are waiting for God and religion.
They are at least skeptical, perhaps antagonistic. In "This Age
of Conformity," Howe offered the classic complaint: the "turn

to religion and religiosity [reflects] the weariness of intellectuals in an age of defeat and their yearning to remove themselves from the bloodied arena of historical action and choice, which necessarily means, of secular action and choice." [21] Podhoretz takes a similar position, regularly attacking what he calls the "church" party in modern literature, accusing it of being a front for an attack on science, industrialism, and liberal democracy, and a weapon of dubious value in the fight against Communism. Theology is only another form of ideology in a day when all ideologies are outmoded. He applauds Camus, who "has visited chaos and returned with the message that all we can do is try to *think* our way back into a world of meaning, to create a new world of meaning that makes no concession to the bankrupt philosophies of church or state." [22] Hyman, who laments our inability to produce an American folk culture because "as a culture we worship nothing in common, and are able to endow no objects with *mana*," [23] is nonetheless quite determined not to go back to the "mana experience" of the past.

> We can never, of course, return to the past, . . . [though the revival of] moribund languages [like Hebrew] . . . seems to be succeeding at least physically. . . . [It] will not bring back . . . Solomon, and will not even solve the traffic problem or wipe out the rural slums. . . . We are inextricably caught up in a civilized condition, and rather than yearning after a return to the past with its meaningful symbols, we must project our real sentimental nostalgia for them into some viable approach to our own time.[24]

So, quite firmly "many of us would call ourselves 'atheist' rather than 'agnostic,' not out of preference for a harsher and more provocative word, but because 'godless' seems a more honest descriptive term than 'unknowing.'" [25]

Here indeed there is room for discussion, if only to clarify the differing emphases of Judaism and Christianity. The unnatural distinction between the sacred and the secular, on the one hand,

and the charge that religious faith can do nothing about traffic jams, on the other, both stem from a view of "religion" that has few roots in Judaism. Dealing with Sholom Aleichem, Howe is brilliantly alive to the Jewish insistence that salvation is as much to be found within history as beyond it, that the love of God must have something to do with making a living, marrying off one's daughters, and making, if not "a world more attractive," then one more reflective of God's rule. The Jewish prophetic tradition demands priority for what Judaism cannot consider a "secular" effort, and the rabbinic tradition gives day-to-day instruction for its implementation. Modern man could use a good dose of both.

This does not mean that Jewish faith can solve every problem, including smog in Los Angeles and poverty in Appalachia, much less the pacification of Red China. Must it? In a settled, stable world, the gap between a sensitivity to ends and the imagination to create fit means might well be less than it is today. Yet in our present desperate situation, to foster a sense of values and the ultimate importance of their pursuit is itself a worthy task and one whose practical consequences might be substantial. And how one can hope to have "*mana* experiences" while remaining resolutely "godless" and seek heroes, rituals, group symbols, cycle-of-the-year celebrations, and mass experiences, as Hyman does, while spurning religion is itself worthy of examination.

The problem of theology as ideology demands a little greater attention, if only to clarify the limits of what Judaism might mean to a modern intellectual. The term "ideology" received its current bad odor in relation to the search for a more realistic liberalism. The classic American liberal had firm opinions about the nature of man, the potential of rationality, and the direction of history. He may not have been as rigid in his theorizing as the Communist, but this commitment was the basis of his political vigor and, as the century wore on, for his seeming naïveté. That liberalism, like the dinosaur, died of inflexibility. If modern man is not to sink into passivity or mysticism and there is to be a new liberalism, it must be far more pragmatic than its predecessor. What Podhoretz wrote in 1958 is still valid:

The most energetic intellectual impulse of the period was pushing toward the idea that the main enemy, both in culture and politics, was the " true believer," the fanatic of whatever complexion, the prisoner of ideology. This being so, the [recent] loss of values could be seen as a positive virtue, a symptom of our progressive liberation from rigid systems of belief. What we in the West stood for was the skeptical empiricist temperament . . . that makes for a healthy political system (since it discourages fanaticism), a prosperous economic life (since it is the basis of technological efficiency), and a flourishing culture (since concreteness is the soul of art).[26]

In the minds of many intellectuals, religion is another ideological straitjacket. A theology that would claim to know the nature of man and the meaning of history must inevitably be doctrinaire. Is that, however, a reasonable characterization of Judaism or of those seeking to create a modern Jewish theology? Christianity centers itself on the search for a redeeming faith and hence must carefully define what belief will or will not save. It has a long though variegated history of dogmas, creeds, and institutional concern with heresy. The nearest thing to a creed that Judaism knows is a song or two, and any effort to assert Jewish authority is met with an argument, as the disputatious commentaries and supercommentaries printed with every Jewish classic show. Dedicated to survival in history so as to redeem it, the Jew sought more to live in holiness than to legislate the theological ground of Jewish existence. Yet though the legal literature is rich in adaptation and diversity, it also proclaims limits and displays a tenacious sense of integrity. Judaism may thus claim to be an unusual fusion of openness to history together with a commitment to its meaning and purpose. Whether such a religion is too rigid for modern man and what the limits of his skeptical stance ought to be are at least worthy of discussion.

The difficulties increase substantially when one turns to the claims that Judaism makes for the significance of the Jewish people. All theological labels aside — chosenness, vocation, Covenant — the Jewish faith proclaims the importance of relating to God as one of this people, serving him through its customs, observing its calendar, remaining loyal to its community, past, present and future — and, if necessary, suffering for its continuity. Without that further commitment to the religious value of the Jewish people, why bother with its differentiating and occasionally handicapping forms of expressing a faith that all now know?

Podhoretz describes the predicament well in reviewing his experience of studying Jewish literature at the Jewish Theological Seminary and seeking to bring to it the same standards he was learning at Columbia. " Jewish literature was either a text, an exhortation, a party platform, or . . . a milestone in the development of Hebrew " to his instructors. Thus, there was always " something impurely partisan or insufferably crude" in their treatment of it.[27] On more mature reflection he concluded:

> The very characteristic I despised in . . . them [his teachers] — their total involvement with their subject, their failure to achieve distance and perspective, their unwillingness even to admit the possibility of detachment — was the only key to a real understanding of Jewishness. . . . For in their view, every Jewish writer presented the same challenge over and over again: what are you going to do about being a Jew? How could I have possibly responded to Bialik when I was not urgently interested in that question? [28]

The place of Jewishness in Judaism is difficult to discuss because of the way in which the writer or critic usually meets it. The only issue of importance to Jews, their ultimate criterion of all things, seems to be, not truth or beauty, but " Is it good for the Jews? " The intellectual is an intellectual because he is dedicated to the cultivation of the broadest knowledge and the most thoughtful judgment. To him this preoccupation with the clan seems a root evil, one which goes against everything for which he stands. There is hardly a critic who has not been scarred by this parochial Jewishness. Howe praises Sholom Aleichem by contrasting him with the reality of Jewish life today. " You find so little idealization, so little of that cozy self-indulgence and special pleading which is the curse of Jewish life." [29] Kazin can consider Malamud's work within the general problem of " ' minority ' writers who have rejected special pleading in favor of modern art." [30] No wonder he waxed enthusiastic over Philip Roth's " Defender of the Faith."

> This is a note that Jews, in writing about other Jews, do not often strike; the appeal to raw human nature, to the individual in his human complexity and loneliness as a mere human creature, is less common than the grand collective themes of Jewish life, of Jewish solidarity in the face of oppression. Even the most gifted and profound writers among Jews tend to describe love and hate, misery and savagery, as if they were merely symbols of the depth and range of Jewish experience. The unusual thing, Mr. Roth's achievement, is to locate the bruised and angry and un-assimilated self — the Jew as individual, not the individual as Jew — beneath the canopy of Jewishness.[31]

Roth is the *cause célèbre* of this clash of values. Again and again [32] he has been asked why such a nice, talented Jewish boy had to write about ugly types in the Jewish community rather than the more ideal sort whom the non-Jew would like. The absolute antipathy any intellectual must feel to such demands is perhaps best given in Saul Bellow's reaction.[33] He bluntly compared this attitude to Khrushchev's standard that good literature is literature that is good for the state. " In literature we cannot accept a political standard. We can only have a literary one." [34]

The defensiveness of the Jewish community is largely a result of the unparalleled disasters that have overtaken world Jewry in recent decades. These have heightened the natural insecurity of a group that has but lately been integrated into the general community, with definite limits at that. What is not often noted is its origins in ambivalence over Jewish identity, and guilt over the present character of Judaism. The American Jew is committed to remaining Jewish — but he isn't really certain why. Such Jewish life as he has managed to create, he knows, would probably not please his grandfather. Hence his Jewish activity, until he reaches an unusually high level of Jewish commitment, is one continuing search for proof that he has been right. Then a famous writer comes along and writes about Jews whom he cannot help rejecting and points out situations in the community of which he cannot approve. Because he cannot deny the truth but does not want to face the negative parts of Jewish life — they are too strong! — he turns on the writer.

The Jewish community cannot hope to speak to the intellectual if it comes only to gain approval. To expect him to tell them why they are right or — that height of American Jewish dedication — to join an organization or institution is to ignore his person for selfish ends. Podhoretz and Roth do not cease to make this clear, and even Fiedler, the self-declared believing Jew among the critics, insists: "One of the most important things for a Jewish writer to do . . . is to stay outside all official Jewish American organizations in the United States." [35] If Jews want the intellectual in the community, they must cherish him for what he is and let him be that. He must always be allowed his distance, judging, criticizing, using his intelligence in a never-ending search for greater honesty and understanding.

Is American Jewry ready for the kind of intellectual give-and-take that has no respect for reputations or position but cares solely for the substance of the thought involved? In private there is no end of evaluation and discussion of every major Jewish figure and program, but no Jewish journal would dare publish a no-holds-barred evaluation of their work. No Jewish book ever gets the hardheaded kind of examination that has made the *New York Review of Books* an intellectual delight, and no paper delivered at a Jewish conference is ever discussed on the floor with nearly the honesty it receives over coffee. If the American Jewish community wants its intellectuals, it must be prepared for criticism, not just window dressing.

The false hopes of the community with its intellectuals come from the folly of seeking the justification of Judaism at the hands of general culture. For over a century now Jewish spokesmen have been preoccupied with the true and necessary doctrine that Judaism can adapt itself to modern society. The result of this steady emphasis has been the impression that the general culture determines the content of Judaism. Its science, its ethics, its aesthetics, set what is true in Judaism. If the intellectual, who represents modern culture, found Judaism meaningful, it would supposedly show that Judaism is a worthy religion for a modern man. The result is doubly the opposite. Having that general culture, serving as one of its leaders, why does the intellectual need that Judaism in any way as it needs him, except perhaps for a few nostalgic reminiscences? To the contrary, having admitted that he speaks from a higher truth, one great enough to judge the truth of Judaism, he often feels safe in condemning it as a matter of general theory. Here it is time to call a halt and let Judaism set its own conditions for meaningful dialogue. These are: equality in discussion, good faith, and appropriate knowledge. The first is obvious, but too often, as the Jewish community sees it, intellectuals who discuss Judaism show neither of the latter two.

When a Jew hates the fact that he is a Jew, no one will ever convince him of the worth of Judaism. Though the outstanding feature of American Jewry in recent years has been its relative self-acceptance, Jewish self-hatred is still common. The Jewish intellectual is often afflicted with it, his success outside Judaism affording him an opportunity to liberate himself from his Jewishness. The very rich — the Baruchs, the Guggenheims, the Gimbels — can escape the stigma of Jewishness by becoming accepted for their money. They have found one way out; the culture heroes have another nearly as good. A generation ago the musicians showed the way, with Koussevitzky and Walter the most obvious examples. Today there is hardly a college campus that does not shelter Jews seeking refuge from their minority origins in the realm of universal intellect. Not to recognize the source of the contempt with which some intellectuals speak of Judaism is to hope for dialogue where what is required is therapy.

Similarly, meaningful discussion of Judaism must be based on intellectual competence, not the assumption of superiority. What indignation would be heard if someone, for instance, were to speak of Shakespeare based on a reading at the age of twelve of a simplified version of Lamb's *Tales from Shakespeare,* an occasional visit to a provincial theater, and the table talk of parents who had once acted in a repertory company but have for years only occasionally attended a play! That is the impression many an intellectual makes when he passes judgment on a Judaism he has not studied since his Bar Mitzvah, nor observed in recent years. The presence of this self-confident ignorance, often joined by an arrogance bred of self-hatred, not pure defensiveness alone, engendered the intense resentment felt by many inside the Jewish community at the famous *Commentary* symposium, " Jewishness and the Younger Intellectuals."

Respect for others, good faith, and knowledge, however, are not lacking in all intellectuals, and certainly not in the men spoken of here. Howe has edited Yiddish stories; Kazin and Bellow have translated them. Podhoretz has studied and taught Hebrew in Hebrew. Fiedler gladly proclaims himself a Jew and seeks to apply his Jewishness in his criticism. Even Hyman, the most peripheral of the group, can be moved to a Jewish tone when, in identifying himself with David Daiches' autobiography, he says, " True, our ancestry is less distinguished, but is not every Jew a king, and do we not all claim descent from Father Abraham, and most of us from the Vilna Gaon in addition? " [36]

Yet even with such men a further condition of dialogue must be asserted. Protagonists of Judaism should no more be required to defend its vulgarization than lovers of literature must justify every semipornographic bid for bestsellerdom. Perhaps there should be a correlation between a high spiritual calling and an elevated taste. The grossness that characterizes much of American Jewry is but one of its many failings which any honest leader will readily acknowledge. But the intrinsic worth of Judaism — that inveterate minority faith — must, in days of nonobservance, be judged more by its ideals than by its pop culture. Not the idolatrous masses of the Divided Kingdom but the handful of prophets who spoke to them determined what was Judaism, though with the decades the people of Israel recognized that they were right and accepted their instruction.

The issue, then, is not why most Jews react defensively to criticism of their community any more than it is why many writers debase their talent in graceless plays for notoriety or money. Rather, what should first be talked about is whether the Jewish assertion of the special significance of the Jews requires a Jewish myopia.

Any doctrine may be betrayed by its followers, but rarely has one been so clearly defined within moral limits and so carefully structured within institutional controls. From the first of the writing prophets on (not to mention the Torah itself), it was iterated and reiterated that choice meant religious service and the judgment of God. Later the rabbinic halachah delineated a way of life that made humility under God's sovereign rule, not arrogance in possession of his law, its recurrent motif. Not Jewish theology but recurrent Jewish suffering is the basis of Jewish defensiveness. Considering the improbable lengths to which its persecutors have been willing to go, must not the judgment of overreaction and oversensitivity be voiced in a compassionate tone?

Doctrinal clarity does not condone but rather condemns the community for effectively silencing the critics on the periphery who challenge its most precious institutions. The prophets after all were neither Jewish organization men nor gentle with their contemporaries. It is difficult to think of an extended passage in which they praised the Israelites for their good works, but from their criticism the Jews were able to draw fresh perspective on their divinely appointed destiny.

The intellectual critic, negative and biting though he may seem, can perform the same function today. Again, Philip Roth is a useful example. People have been so busy enjoying or decrying Roth's beautifully written, revealing depictions of Jews that they have failed to take note of his moral power. Though he claims that he desires only to write, not to instruct, Roth's genius burns best when it serves a transcendent ideal. The contrast between the Patimkins' attitude to Neil and his to the young Negro in *Goodbye, Columbus*, Marx's slow shift from the Throne of Mercy to that of Justice in "Defender of the Faith," the humbling of dogmatic arrogance before the commitment to life in "The Conversion of the Jews," are all prophetic denunciations of modern Jewish practice in the name of a higher, if unspoken, truth. The relative failures of "You Can't Tell a Man by the Song He Sings" and "Eli, the Fanatic" stem in large measure from the blunting of the indictment and the tentativeness of the moral affirmation. After his two unsatisfactory novels it is fair to ask whether Roth can fulfill his gifts as a writer except in service of a prophetic vision. (It would, of course, help if Philip Roth's soul and style, inseparable, permitted him to identify more with his Jewish characters. As Howe says of Sholom Aleichem's popularity, despite his unsparing eye for the frailties of the Jews, they loved each other, and "having love, they had no need for politeness.")[37]

Leaving aside, then, all the shadow issues of the intellectual's self-hatred and the Jew's self-interest, is it possible for a modern man to believe that the people of Israel has a special role in history? Or, to put it more broadly, is truth really to be found in particular or universal form? Is the outreach to all cultures, all philosophies, all visions of life's meaning, more likely to produce a greater measure of truth than first grounding oneself firmly in that of Judaism?

These are legitimate, fundamental questions. What must be said of them is that they are not yet foreclosed, for much of the drive of contemporary thought provides new ways of responding to them. The past decade or so has heard one long continuing cry that the individual has become lost in his generalizations. The intellectual task of the day is the recovery of the individual, of particularity, of concreteness, without losing the ethical benefits that universalizing thought about human behavior has produced.

This is true in politics, psychology, and literature; why is it not equally true in religion? The Jewish teaching that universalism can be realized only in the Messianic Age, though it must be fostered and anticipated in historic particularities, seems to the modern Jew a realistic fusion of the two attitudes. At least the issue is discussible, and that is all that is at stake here.

The final matter is one of will. With so much effort required on both sides to make communication possible, why should either undertake it? The Jewish response comes quite easily. The community has always prized intellectuality, and in its present perilous position it needs as much intellectual help as it can find. If today intelligence makes itself felt in criticism rather than in system-building or guidance-giving, then Jews should not forget how much they have benefited from such negative formulations in the past when they were able to accept them less in pique than in self-transcendence. There is always the hope that the intellectual may move on to make positive contributions to the shaping of a fulfilled American Judaism, though that seems more likely at the moment in the arts than in literature. Primarily, however, Jews might gain the stimulation of the intellectual's companionship, not at the meetings of Jewish organizations — that becomes increasingly almost too great a sacrifice to ask of deeply committed Jews! — but in one or another of the many simple personal ways that go to make up Jewish life. He is another interesting person-Jew, both at once, and it would be nice to be able to talk with him about mutual concerns. Why he, in turn, should make the effort to inquire or respond he must answer for himself. From the point of view of Judaism it might help him fill out the dimensions of his life as person and as Jew.

These intellectuals affirm the dignity of man and the worth of his moral endeavor, but they do not probe the ground of their assurance. The anomaly of a rootless moral passion is not unknown to them. Howe has written:

The search for moral style is recurrent in modern writing. It places a great burden upon literature, almost the burden of demanding that literature provide us with norms of value we find unable to locate in experience. It tends to demand from literature a kind of prophetic gratification which would have seemed decidedly strange to earlier generations of readers.[38]

Judaism has something important to say about the beginnings and the ends of human striving. While it may not have final, absolute answers to many questions, it can provide a measure of guidance and direction that would help integrate lives already too fragmentized.

Judaism has something to say, too, about their Jewish existence, divided as it is between acceptance of their identity and an inability to know what to do with it. How many of the values on which they are building their lives came to them out of a particular Jewish setting and, while they may be considered the property of all mankind, are still particularly prized and fostered in the Jewish community? As Hyman notes:

> Ultimately, perhaps, more than historical and linguistic identification, Jewish identity is habits of mind, patterns of taste. . . . But these . . . are not inherited, they were trained in Daiches by the study of Talmud and Torah. Will his children have them? Will their children? . . . We . . . may yet find that with the best will in the world, timeless Jewish cultural identity without time-bound Jewish ritual . . . diminishes and attenuates over the years and the generations.[39]

Why, even their skill as literary critics, as Hyman perceives, may well have its roots in the generations who bequeathed to them a love for and a sensitivity to a text. "Like so many skewed Talmudists, Daiches is a specialist in the rabbinic niceties of literary criticism. . . . [He] remembers the characteristic form of discourse in his household to have been argument." [40]

What is the meaning of their experience projected on a larger scale? That some sons of immigrant generations should succeed seems natural. That so many have is worthy of some special sociological note. That generations of Jews have managed to live in creative sanctity over centuries under the most diverse circumstances, however, is a matter productive of awe. If these men could see their Jewish lives significantly in terms of Jewish history and destiny, they would understand themselves far better and with a greater sense of integrity. At least, so it would seem to the believing Jew.

With this greater wholeness as man-Jew, they might add new depth to their critical perception. Much has been written about the possibilities of a Christian literary criticism. No one has investigated the ways in which Judaism might enable the critic to bring special sensitivity to a task that so often involves the values by which men ought to live. Leslie Fiedler [41] may illustrate this possibility, for he has brought to much of his work an outspoken commitment to his Jewishness, largely through what he understands to be its doctrine of *galut*, or alienation. Thus, not only his essays on the success of recent American Jewish writers but also his discussions of the Negro novel and the future of American fiction show the benefit of his effort to remain a Jewish " outsider " to modern culture. The point is not whether Fiedler's avowal of his Jewishness makes him a better critic than Hyman, Kazin, *et al.* A well-developed sense of human values is not all the equipment a critic needs. When he has mastered his techniques, done his homework, and knows his art, he may well benefit from a living relation to a tradition that deepens and unifies his feel for human existence. Fiedler's appropriation of the " Jew as alien " motif hardly exhausts Judaism. Jews have also known how to participate in society without losing their identity and how to work and " wait for the end " (a Hebraic term, despite Fiedler's citation of Empson) as well as to bemoan their alien lot.

Despite these possibilities, what if, in Podhoretz' poignant words, the intellectuals " are no longer urgently interested in that question "? What if they do not want to talk, or, talking, want out? Are not indifference and rejection — the former more than the latter — the most realistic expectations of this quest for communication, even when pursued by the Jewish community in the fullest maturity and self-respect? That is the price one must pay for living in *galut*. (Nor is the State of Israel any less *galut*, as the flight of its writers from "ghetto" values into the international style shows.) This sad expectation does not lessen the community's responsibility to seek its children but requires that the motive for such outreach be based on inner love, not outer response.

The pain of such continual loss must not depress those within the community to the point where they despair over Judaism and its ultimate destiny. For all its love of intellectuality, the Jewish people is kept alive by God, not by the approval of the cultural leaders of the age. He has not shown himself daunted by the need to use the ordinary and the simple, the infirm and the unstable, for his historic purposes. He has managed over the centuries to find his own intellectuals. In brotherly Jewish stubbornness, let it be said, he may yet be using those distant from his people to remind the faithful remnant of their unceasing responsibilities.

That puts Jewish faith where it belongs, in God, and not in the general culture and its heroes. This is the most important task the Jew has, even in his outreach to the intellectuals. It is ever again to find and live his Jewish faith, for if there were many Jews who authentically exemplified Judaism, conversation with the intellectuals or anyone else who wanted to know about Judaism would be far easier — or hardly even necessary.

NOTES: *Chapter 9*

1. Irving Howe and Eliezer Greenberg (eds.), *A Treasury of Yiddish Stories* (The Viking Press, Inc., 1954). See p. 2 and *passim*.

2. Norman Podhoretz, *Doings and Undoings* (Farrar, Straus & Co., 1964), p. 124.

3. Stanley Edgar Hyman, *The Promised End: Essays and Re-*

views, 1942–1962 (The World Publishing Company, 1963), p. 12.

4. Alfred Kazin, *Contemporaries* (Little, Brown and Company, 1962), p. 507.

5. *Ibid.*, p. 501.

6. Hyman, *op. cit.*, p. 354.

7. *Ibid.*, p. 355.

8. *Ibid.*, p. 371.

9. Kazin, *op. cit.*, pp. 207, 213.

10. *Ibid.*, p. 216.

11. *Ibid.*, p. 495.

12. Irving Howe, in his book *A World More Attractive* (Horizon Press, 1963).

13. Podhoretz, *op. cit.*, p. 3.

14. *Ibid.*, p. 259.

15. *Ibid.*, p. 264.

16. Howe, *op. cit.*, p. 207.

17. Hyman, *op. cit.*, p. 346.

18. Kazin, *op. cit.*, p. 207.

19. *Ibid.*, pp. 207, 262, 182, 185, 189, 254.

20. Podhoretz, *op. cit.*, p. 242.

21. Howe, *op. cit.*, p. 272.

22. Podhoretz, *op. cit.*, p. 171.

23. Hyman, *op. cit.*, pp. 271–272.

24. *Ibid.*, p. 276.

25. *Ibid.*, p. 335.

26. Podhoretz, *op. cit.*, pp. 161 f. See also the ongoing debate in *Commentary* beginning with Henry David Aiken's article "The Revolt Against Ideology," April, 1964, the correspondence on it, Sept., 1964, and the fracas with Daniel Bell, Oct., 1964.

27. Podhoretz, *op. cit.*, p. 119.

28. *Ibid.*, pp. 122 f.

29. Howe, *op. cit.*, p. 215.

30. Kazin, *op. cit.*, p. 202.

31. *Ibid.*, p. 259.

32. "Writing About Jews," *Commentary*, Dec., 1963, and the extensive correspondence, April, 1964. More usefully, the *Con-*

gress Bi-Weekly report of the " Second Dialogue in Israel," Sept. 16, 1963.

33. Saul Bellow (ed.), *Great Jewish Short Stories* (Dell Publishing Company, Inc., 1963).

34. *Ibid.,* p. 14.

35. *Congress Bi-Weekly,* p. 59.

36. Hyman, *op. cit.,* p. 334.

37. Howe, *op. cit.,* p. 215.

38. *Ibid.,* p. 75.

39. Hyman, *op. cit.,* p. 340.

40. *Ibid.,* p. 335.

41. Leslie A. Fiedler, *Waiting for the End* (Stein and Day, Inc., Publishers, 1964).

Chapter

10

CONFRONTING THE SECULAR
AT THE UNIVERSITY

Perhaps some members of the clergy can still avoid the question of religion's relationship to the secular style of existence. Clerical bureaucrats or local officiants may have their lives so fully integrated with their institutions that they can ignore or simply do not see what is moving in general society. The campus teacher of religion is too exposed to escape even if he teaches in a religiously oriented institution. He may hide from secularity, but it will come and seek him out. Something has happened — and it seems irreversible.

He sees it most clearly in his students. They look at him differently than they used to. They listen, but not as they once did. There was a day when they regularly expected to be told what to believe. So the clergy told them and that generally satisfied them. If they questioned but the matter was not critical, they were satisfied to accept the answers given them. They had respect for authority and assumed that it had a legitimate role to play in their education.

That somewhat idealized picture of the past still holds true of many students, but they are no longer the mood-making group. More interesting, even their teachers question their attitude. They seem, somehow, too passive, too accepting. Can they really be mature if they do not assert themselves in argument? if they do not criticize and challenge? if they do not seek to exercise their autonomy?

That is the key term for secular man: autonomy. He is determined to be man for himself, to find his own way, to come to his own conclusions. That is why he looks and listens differently. He may be deeply determined to accept the guidance of religion, to recognize that it possesses a wisdom and competence that he can never own without its help. Still, he wants to take his personal resources as far as he can. As long as he can think, question, wonder, reason, he is not ready for authority. He wants explanations, analyses, validations, at least discussion. He does not want simply to be told the truth. He is not ready for conclusions until he has taken his search to the limits of his capacities, and perhaps not then, for he knows he will almost certainly renew the quest tomorrow. Such decisions as he will make he considers a private, highly personal matter so only he, not another, may say when it is time for him to stop examining and make a commitment. Only he may say when and what he is willing to believe.

That is what autonomy means and that is what secularity is teaching today's children, youth, and adults. They have rights, real rights, in their study of religion as in anything else. Moreover, insofar as the representatives of religion do not grant them their rights, they know the teachers have indicated they cannot teach them God's truth. Although secularity may have taught them the fundamental necessity of the struggle for autonomy, it is clear to them that its foundation is already to be found in Biblical faith. Each man is precious, for he is created in God's image. Each man has capacities for understanding and believing, and they are what dignify him as man. Each man has a conscience whose dictates he is bound to obey, even as he is responsible for sensitizing and informing it. Then insofar as he strives to be what he was created to be, he must exert himself to appropriate what, as best he can, he finds to be the truth. Not to do so is to be less a man, even not a man, in both secular and religious eyes.

So students today are skeptical where once they were accepting, and questioning where once they would have acquiesced. They

are, at their best, active not passive, self-determining not con-
formist, independent not subservient.

Of course that is too great a burden for most of them. They
aspire to autonomy but they are afraid of its responsibilities and
probably afraid of some mythical power religion may have to
strike them dead. So they don that impregnable modern arma-
ment: politeness. They are respectful and courteous. They are
quiet but they also do not thereby signify agreement. They sit
there with question marks behind their half-open eyes wondering
whether their teachers really believe what they are saying, how
they act when they are alone or with their peers, whether they
can carry on a knock-down, drag-out argument with a well-in-
formed skeptic — and so forth. Regardless of what they answer
on examination papers, who knows what they really believe?

They are increasingly a new breed. Though they may have
been born in a faith and trained and nurtured in it, when they
come to study it on a college level they want to approach it with
the same dispassionate, critical stance they bring to all their other
serious study. That is how real religion's confrontation with secularity is, for secularity now sets the very tone and style in which
the intellectual examination of religion itself must proceed. Even
within a religious institution, dealing with a student body which
almost certainly chose this school because of its religious character, and even in the courses on its faith, indeed, as should be
obvious by now, even in seminary courses on theology, the new
secular skepticism makes itself increasingly felt. No wonder, then,
that the college teacher who would ignore this growing change
of mood must either have a chair at Shangri-la University or else
have not faced anything but his research for several years. At the
secular university what is masked elsewhere becomes the *sine qua
non* of instruction.

Secularity often means a good deal more than a commitment
to autonomy and much of it takes forms far less positive than
students' desires to think religious matters through for themselves.
Still, examining it in this particular locus brings to the surface
the hidden agenda behind such current catch phrases as "The

world has come of age," " God is dead," and " the post-Christian era." When the student is seen as secular man at his most self-conscious and when his instructor believes in the faith he is discussing, then the confrontation of religion with secularity is made immediate and direct. Such a situation makes obvious the conclusion that if religion is to say anything meaningful to large numbers in our time — and perhaps today it can only speak in an authentic way to a small minority — it must somehow learn to speak in terms of the secular style of the age. Though there is much that is troublesome in the current confusion called theology, later ages will not be able to accuse some sizable minority of religious men of attempting to do just that. They are seeking honestly, often radically, to grasp the meaning of what their society is going through and to respond to it. They may turn out to have been wrong, even foolish, in their desperate effort to communicate. They would prefer that judgment to one that would accuse them of the irresponsibility of inaction in an age seething with change and in a society marching to agnosticism or worse.

The first barrier to useful confrontation, then, is the willingness of religion to reach out to the secular style of the day. That conceded, the problems, as usual, only begin. With whom shall one speak and how can one do so? The questions sound so simple. The social and philosophic realities are annoyingly complex.

In organized religion one might hope to find authorized spokesmen — though it is remarkable to what an extent what once looked like carefully structured and defined faiths have in recent years shown themselves to be extraordinarily flexible and changing. Yet where shall one go if one wishes to open an ecumenical institute with contemporary secularity? The Communist Party certainly enshrines one aspect of it and that is what has made the exchanges between Christians and Communists so interesting. But Western secularity is not only not essentially communistic, it may well be said to be postcommunistic. When Communism was believable, it served as a substitute absolute for the irreligious man. When the communist god failed, that was the practical end of all absolutes and the beginning of postmodern secularist realism, namely, that ideolgies are per se bad, that final answers are unobtainable, that provisional responses to human situations are all men can hope for, that a healthy skepticism toward all human activities is the beginning of wisdom.

That is why one perhaps should refer to secularity as a style or mood. It is not organized or socially structured, though it pervades the culture. It is not a program or a creed. Then who is one to talk to if one wishes to confront secularity? The answer must be, why, everyone who shares fully in our civilization or, if we wish secularity at its best, those who lead the culture, whoever they are — which is just the problem.

If there is any place where secularity is institutionalized, it is the modern university. Willy-nilly it proclaims and powers the secular style. Though its curriculum contains no required courses on secularity, one of its most widespread activities is the conversion of its students to the secular approach to things. If that were altogether a bad thing, it would be the greatest argument known for complete education under religious auspices. Since the secular style is to a considerable extent, even from the religious standpoint, good and desirable, however, religion cannot simply oppose it. Indeed, that is why as religious-sponsored universities pursue quality and high standards they too must inevitably absorb much of the secular approach to things. That, too, is why as higher education grows in this country one may confidently expect society's commitment to secularity to increase.

The other place where one might hope to meet the significant secularists is in the loose confederation of persons, journals, and institutions that give leadership to our high culture and, in particular, our influential critics and writers, the literary establishment. But whether one reaches out to professors or to literati, the distinctive response is: They are not interested. They are reasonably certain, particularly since the postwar revival of religion — may it rest in peace — caused them to take another look at it, that religion has nothing to say to them. They aren't anticlerical or passionately atheistic. Either would be a form of religious hang-up. They just don't care. For them, not just God but religion is dead.

Religion today faces secular triumphalism, so it should not be too optimistic about the results of such confrontation with secularity as it might manage. The overwhelming majority of people find it as natural to ignore religious coffeehouses, theological folk singers, and jazz liturgy as they did conventional religious activities. If the purpose in this outreach is dramatically to reverse statistics, then church and synagogue are doomed to heartbreak and a speedy return to religious reaction.

Realistically, then, the primary area of contact with secularity is likely to be with students in religion courses or in religious-sponsored colleges. To them must be added all those many adults who these days read and hear theologians. One confronts secularity most directly in the questions, the concerns, and the criteria they bring to discussions with them. When the teacher cares and the students, perhaps only for the sake of inquiry, assume the stance of critical questioners, there the dialogue is as real as, from the stance of faith, it is poignant.

That formal situation imposes on the protagonists of religion a special burden with regard to recognizing the students' autonomy, for the teacher and his student are not equals. The class must sit quietly while he speaks until the one side of a supposed communication between persons has run its extended length. Then they are, most often, permitted only to answer his questions. Should they in independence challenge him radically, he has the height of his platform, the freedom from time limits, and the privilege of having the last word with which to overwhelm his challenger. In a class setting, the teacher is virtually omnipotent. He has maturity, advanced education, examinations, and eventually graduation, to use against his students. If he is a clergyman, he teaches, so it seems, with God's authority behind him.

What often happens, then, in this sinful world of ours, is that autonomous inquiry is often met with power rather than with fair-minded intellectual exchange. Yet if a teacher violates the autonomy of his students in their relationship, then he cannot hope to teach them anything about true faith. How can the students take the teacher and his teaching about religion seriously when he does not really treat them like persons? Since students are sensitive to and suspicious of religious leaders perhaps beyond all others of the older generation, they are always watching to see if the pious will abuse their power.

That does not mean that they, in defense of their independence, want all proponents of religion to be their buddies or chums. That would be as false to the teacher as a person as it is to the reasons that brought the students to the class. They came to find persons who are supposed to have superior wisdom or at least unusual competence in the nature of religious belief. That gap in knowledge, they know, rightly grants the faculty special status, so what they ask is not pedagogic egalitarianism but only that they not be denied their rights as persons.

That insidious temptation somehow transcended, how does one proceed with the intellectual task of confronting secularity?

Here again differences multiply, for just as there is no definable institutional focus for secularity in our culture, so it has no agreed-upon intellectual content. It is, apparently, more a cultural mood than a single philosophic language. That is one reason why religious men spend so much time arguing about the true nature of secularity — the irony being that their debate is with other religious men. If, to take an easy example, communist-style materialism spoke for modern secularity, then religious men could devote their energies to understanding its terms, to translating religion into them wherever possible and questioning its assumptions where they could not. The greater difficulty is that pluralism is the chief characteristic of secular intellectuality. It might well represent itself via atheistic existentialism or phenomenology or philosophy of science or linguistic analysis. Each has been proclaimed by some theoretician the language par excellence of the modern world. The responsibility of the religious thinker is to know all these secular philosophies, to appreciate their appeal and then seek to meet their challenge in all its particularity.

Often, if the secular philosopher's rejoinders are taken with full seriousness, one must admit that the issue remains in doubt, sometimes in his favor. It is important not to hesitate to admit this, to oneself and to one's students. Often such mental crossroads mean that a fundamental choice of values or sense of vision has been reached. Confronting this decision will help one clarify alternative criteria of judgment and different approaches to life. Religion may not be the only way but in the divergence it emerges in its distinctiveness. Here the student may come to recognize that he shares its choices, though other parts of his life, hopefully the less ultimate, may better be understood under the rubrics of secular philosophy.

That leads to another level of the confrontation. Religion cannot simply remain passive before the demands of a triumphant secularity. To see these confrontations as religion's efforts to explain itself in secular terms is to make of the older partner in the meeting a servile and dependent thing. Religion, too, is entitled to make its demands and ask its questions. It, too, must have autonomy or else there can be no meaningful discussion. It must therefore issue its own challenges to secularist intellectuals and these may most usefully be two in number. The first is directed toward the secularist's sense of certainty.

Why are they so certain that that which they define as alone making sense or being reasonable is the only proper way in which meaning can be considered meaning? The question presents itself because religious assertions are regularly asked to present themselves before the bar of secular categories of judgment and then are often told that they have no significant content. Some religious men have struggled valiantly then to reinterpret religious teaching in such a way as to qualify as meaningful within these restricted terms — think of Braithewaite's lecture, "An Empiricist View of the Nature of Religious Belief" and, in another way, Dewart's *The Future of Belief*. Others have sought to modify the secularist categories so as to accommodate religious concepts better — Van Buren's *The Secular Meaning of the Gospel*, and Teilhard de Chardin's *The Phenomenon of Man* easily come to mind. Yet the former efforts result in very substantial compromises with traditional faith and the latter, despite the religious compromises, are generally rejected by secularist theoreticians.

Why should religious men not directly challenge any narrow concept of rationality, that is, any form that makes it by definition impossible or impractical for religious men to speak of their faith? Reason and rationality have not meant the same thing in all periods of philosophy. If historicism has made religious men humble about giving fixed, permanent, objective statements of the content of their faith, it should equally keep philosophers from being dogmatic about the necessary meaning of reason. The contemporary philosophic world is sufficiently pluralistic about what constitutes evidence and requires conviction that the claims of one philosophic style versus another cannot be asserted over against religion without serious challenge as to the source of its own certainty.

The point of this religious counterquestioning of secularity is not to demonstrate the validity of religion. Rather, in exposing the dogmatic roots of the philosophy that stands over against religion in judgment, it may hope to clarify the common fundamental problems of religious and philosophic assumptions. By so doing it may render what was the unequal contest of an outworn mysticism against a contemporary rationalism into a dialogue between two tentative, highly personal, and problematic efforts to search for significant truth.

Another area in which religion should take the polemic tack is the ground of ethics. The secularist's dearest hope is that he can have the best of religion — ethics — without its faith in God or its institutional concretizations. It is the unethical conduct of religious men and institutions that forms one of his chief weapons against religion's validity. He is, by contrast, happy to point out the many ethical men who are nonetheless atheists and agnostics. On both counts religious men have had to give humble assent. They have sinned and others have often, without any claim to faith, been far more virtuous. Indeed, because of this prophetic secular judgment, religious men have resolved to be better, more active exemplars of their faith and that has changed the complexion of contemporary religious life.

That is no reason not to ask, particularly with an eye toward the future, whence the secularist will derive his ethical impetus as the current tide of secularity swells to full strength. What doctrine or institutions will supply the kind of ethical motivation that will make men strive to be humane and will cause them to work and suffer to make their society fully decent? If religion is as hardheaded and realistic about secularity as secularity has been about religion, it is beyond belief that the secular world, as currently visible, can move significantly beyond moral neutralism. The intellectual bases either for a strong doctrine of natural law or some sort of Kantian moral law have been thoroughly eroded by modern skepticism. No philosophy today empowers and elevates conscience, while economics, sociology, psychology, and particularly psychoanalysis make men distrustful of it. If it is the personal on which men seek to base their ethics, why should men, particularly the strong and able, care for persons, particularly the weak and unattractive? How can anyone have a simple faith in human nature or the goodness of the interhuman when recent history has been one continuous revelation of man's unbelievable capacity for barbarism? Moreover, if man's perversity is so great and if his society is so dominated by self-interest and the will to power as we have at such pain come to know, then it is not a little utilitarian accommodationism that the times require, but tough, determined, unyielding devotion to the traditional moral values.

Again, the point of this counterthrust is not to prove religion right by showing the moral vacuity of contemporary secularity. In all such arguments leading to an either/or choice the man who is moved to decision is as likely to take the "either" of nihilism to the "or" of religion. That is quite a risk indeed. Yet the hope of this tactic would again be to deprive the secularist of his prima facie sense of superiority over religion, before which meaningful discussion is most unlikely. If he can come to see that secularity might entail a loss of ethical substance and drive, he will at least be struck by his own problematic which may then loom as great as religion's. If he has firm faith in the fundamental signification of ethical action, there may be a basis upon which he and the religious man can begin mutually to speak of the nature and ground of commitments. The quality of the discussion will then be altered, perhaps made possible for the first time.

The temptation involved in such polemics is very great. The audience, one must remember, is essentially the unsophisticated, the semireligious, if not the convinced. How easy it is before them to score victories against the heathen secularists! But if these refutations are quick and crushing, if the day is carried by flashy rhetoric or the exercise of clerical authority, nothing is won, for everyone knows that the opponent was not present and had he been, religion might not only have sounded less convincing but have been soundly rebuffed. If, then, such a discussion is to be meaningful to students and accomplish religion's task of confronting secularity through their struggle with it, then it must be treated, in the absence of its representatives, with great respect. Every such discussion must show an openness to secularity's truths, a willingness to accept its criticisms, a knowledge of its arguments at their best, and only then present a patient, thoughtful statement of opposition. That is not the end of the matter, for it must be followed in turn by a consideration of such replies to the religious criticism that would likely be made.

The issue is almost less the substance of the confrontation than its style and that, more than what is said, will be of importance to those who are involved in it. Two things are demanded to authenticate any religious presentation: realism and openness. Both presume high intellectuality but go beyond it.

Secular men will reject any public truth that contradicts what they know is a private reality. They know religion has been and is corrupt, while religious men have been and are full of doubt. They have been trained to face the glandular, monetary, class, and power realities of life. They are against all illusion, if they are moderns, and they will resent the use of sentimentality, nostalgia, or an appeal to tradition is a substitute for reasoning. If religious men cannot face up to reality as moderns have increasingly come to know it, then their faith is an infantile escape, an abandonment of responsibility fit only for the weak and immature.

This does not mean that students of religion want the clergy to use obscene language or theologians to show off what they have finally found out life is all about. The students would prefer their teachers to know but then transcend all that in a way that shows the practicality of faith ennobling man. They see the relevance and significance of religion most clearly when its ideals are shown to apply precisely to the grimy, gritty world of everyday and not merely to the sanctuary or academy.

That is partly what is involved in openness, but the point must be developed somewhat further. One of the astonishing discoveries of modern man is that the unthinkable alternative often turns out to have much to teach us. To close out discussion before a position has been thoughtfully considered has become a major methodological error. " There may be something to it " is often the beginning of insight. In the field of religion discussion has often been prevented and foreclosed. What seems anathema or heresy, it has been reasoned, should not, except at the hand of skilled polemicists, receive consideration. Today's students expect far more of theologians. They will take it as a sign of a teacher's insecurity in faith or thought if he refuses to consider seriously contrary possibilities of belief and concept and is not open to question, argument, and challenge.

Above all they expect openness to the teacher's as well as the students' limitations. They know no one knows the whole of God's truth in final form, and they hope their instructors know they do not know it all. A believer hopefully has enough faith to be pleasing in God's sight but his understanding of that faith in this complex, confusing age must surely have an open, questing texture. Even the informed must be striving to know more and better what they believe, must have their questions and their doubts. So they should be open to the fragile nature of their students' web of commitments and denials of this moment. They, too, want to grow and develop, but they wish to do so in their own way. They want to come to faith autonomously. Hence they do not want to be rushed, pushed, manipulated, or catapulted. They want their teachers to be open to their doubt and their quest, and they do not want anyone to force conclusions upon them. They want all instructions therefore to climax at the most in a question left with them for them to answer, without compulsion, in their own way. That does not mean, all the alternatives considered, that there is no room for the teacher to state, even with some passion, what he considers to be true or what he believes his religion requires and why. Still, he must leave them with the right to decide. Even while pressing his view he must respect their autonomy.

The religiously committed instructor teaches to bring men to faith or to make them surer in it. They, the students of a secular world, study in order to have a basis for their own, quite private commitments. The one group wants converts, partisans, vocations. The other wants to hear as much as they can and in the quiet movement of their own souls make their decisions. The one hopes to convince. The other studies to consider.

That is the emotion-ridden challenge of secularity to the believing teacher of religion. Modern man insists upon his rights to his own decisions. He will, at best, listen. Then, considering religion as one of many disciplines speaking to his soul, he will make up his own mind as to what he will do. He wants teachers of religion to state their faith as best they can, but then leave the issue of his decision with him in all openness. He will see — and that is where his sense of the usefulness of religious instruction ends.

Can the teacher who cares about his faith be content to leave matters there, knowing full well that if he seeks to do more than simply to present his view he will alienate his student? How can he give his heart and soul and might to his faith and remain content not finally to bring the other to it? How can he leave the future of his belief in such a precarious state and not strive on until he has won another generation for that which he believes is ultimately true?

The rise of secularity has, in fact, changed what one can hope to accomplish by teaching doctrine. Intellectual formulations will, at best, make the autonomous decision for faith possible. In an age dominated by skepticism and negativism that is no small accomplishment, particularly since without that intellectual clarification it is difficult to believe that modern man could commit himself to anything. But insofar as religious faith has become a matter of the most personal, private decision, it will be far more affected by models than by argument. Here who the men of faith are and what religion shows forth are the most effective means of making its impress on a secular world. Are believers persons? Do they respect persons, even when they have power over them? Do they work and struggle and risk for the fate of persons in our society and world? These are the questions secular man is asking of religion.

If the faithful are frightened by the inadequacy of their theology and the insufficiency of their lives before this intense secular scrutiny, then they should remember the destiny of religion is not in their hands. It is not they, responsible as they must be, who must ultimately keep alive and sustain religious faith, but God himself. It is because they trust in him that they can face the anxiety of this new open-texturedness which the secular age demands of the teaching of religion. They are required to continue to try in their faltering way to serve his purposes because he has regularly chosen to use the simple and the ordinary as the instruments of his working. Without his help how could they hope to do his work in this world? With his help they may hope, in his own good time, to see even a world suffused with secularity become the place of his Kingdom.

Chapter

11

SECULAR CONSCIENCE AND
ORGANIZED RELIGION

For a century or more now, Judaism and Christianity have been criticized intensively by secular ethics. From this process they have learned or at least have become sensitive to the fact that internal autocracy creates subservience not righteousness, and justifying social evil as God's will perpetuates exploitation not virtue. Synagogue and church now know they must practice if they hope to preach and show themselves nobler than ordinary institutions if they claim to represent more than man.

Secular man is blunt about his demands. They proceed from his fundamental commitment: to reject illusion and accept reality, no matter how bitter. Religious men find this hardheadedness, particularly when applied to their actions, difficult to accept yet impossible to reject. Under the secular tones sound the echoes of Israel's ancient prophets asking God's people to sacrifice their pretensions as they stand before his altar-throne of judgment.

That is why some religious men today are anxious to make an alliance with secularity. They assume that it still has the ethical initiative and that religion, by such amalgamation, would find new power for its ancient ethical aspirations.

In part that is surely true. Religious institutions are not nearly yet models of corporate righteousness and in many cases they remain silent partners, perhaps even participants in every sort of human deprivation and exploitation. " We sin; we transgress; we do perversely " — so much so that God's judgment is rarely spoken within religious institutions but must be heard from secular prophet critics. That sinfulness is real. Before men pretense might yet be possible. Before God only repentance is appropriate.

Yet while religious men should be grateful to secularity for refreshing their ethical sensitivity, the time has come to return the favor. Apply to it the same sort of hardheaded, realistic analysis it has brought to religion, demythologize it, and the conclusion is clear — modern secularity is ethically bankrupt. Conscience, if by that is meant anything like the Biblical sense of humane existence, is decaying in the contemporary technical civilization. The more secularity seeks to be consistent with its anti-transcendent bent, the less it seems able to power moral existence. Such feeble conscience as it does engender is incommensurate with the vast human power it continues to unleash.

That judgment is made not because there are no longer individual saints in technopolis but rather in terms of the major forces — political, economic, social — which realistically shape civilization.

The American democracy is an incredibly great human achievement, yet it can only be expected to create politicians not moralists. Even the best of political men must shape his life in terms of power not conscience. To gain or maintain offices he will bend the truth, halve the truth, deny the truth. Publicly he may pretend to virtue. Privately he will be ruthless — that is why we are so interested in memoirs about him. The greatness of democracy is not its ability to produce men of conscience but its harnessing of their drive to power for the common welfare. Civil servants who take moral stands in the face of the power realities are a joy precisely because they are abnormally courageous. Politics is a power game. To expect it to encourage devotion to ethics is naïve.

The American corporation, the pinnacle of our financial system, is a marvel of human cooperation, but its concern is profit not character. A good executive will show economic not moral initiative. If he wants to get to the executive suite, he will not carry on within the company an uneconomic fight for pure air, safe cars, or reasonably priced drugs. If corporations are more community-minded in recent years, this is a roundabout way of making money by enhancing image. Economics thinks in fiscal terms. To expect it to create conscience is delusion.

Our social order is extraordinarily open, yet it is based on the perpetuation of privilege. At its height is the club. There one meets one's status peers. But the condition of this accomplishment is the exclusion of others, the prerequisite of membership conformity to the establishment. Conscience is an impediment to the climber, morality a brake on upward mobility. Yet the lower classes feel equal antimoral pressures. Increasing urbanization concentrates degradation. This is modified with just enough welfare to smother revolution but not enough to give real hope. The social ladder, up or down, leads to no moral heaven.

These political, economic, and social orders are, at least, amoral; hence, by Biblical standards, they are immoral. So man hoped that our educational institutions might produce a countervailing ethical empetus. However, the university, that industry of intellectuality, does not transmit humanism as much as program technicians. Only freshman expect to gain moral wisdom in class and they are soon educated to reality. Then, more maturely, they work to beat the system, to get credits, deferments, recommendations, jobs, spouses. Their teachers cooperate in this disengagement, for they in turn want grants, promotions, appointments, status, and these come by way of astute politics based on publishable research, not by molding character. Of course, there are great teachers and good schools, but mostly that means making knowledgeable specialists interestingly. There is also a tiny minority on campus today who are America's most active ethical secularists. Yet their idealism, as their numbers show, is based, not institutionally, but privately (of which more below). As long as the university models itself after industry and depends upon the generosity of government it may not realistically be expected to make moral activity its goal.

High culture might once have been education's surrogate. Once the great authors set a model of moral striving before the age. Today our book, stage, movie, and television writers are moral heroes if they merely avoid the blandishments of the million-dollar markets. Amid the entertainers and the titillaters, the foes of illusion and the prophets of nihilism, a positive voice is rarely heard. Most writers cannot even affirm aesthetic forms, much less moral standards. Were the culture morally ripe, is it still believable in a post-Nazi era that aesthetic experiences easily transform the ethical realities of existence?

To shift the focus from social to individual forces will not help. Psychiatry, the most helpful of the personal sciences, is having enough difficulty meeting its therapeutic responsibilities to be burdened with promoting ethics. Besides, its very methods militate against such a success. Behind the fearsome standards of human conduct, it discloses, is the fear of father. Let the neurotic subservience to a despotic superego dissolve, and authority can nevermore claim an unquestioned obedience. So today when men become emotionally involved in moral matters they wonder what unconscious factors have reasserted themselves and made them "lose their cool." True, now an autonomous devotion to ethics would be created that would be the most appropriate foundation for ethical living. That task, however, is more metaphysical than psychodynamic and as much beyond the practical scope as the intellectual competence of psychiatry.

Then some hope simply to put their trust in man, supposing that if he were brought up in family love and a noncompetitive social order his innate goodness would assert itself! Such sentimentality used to be a characteristic of religious thinkers; what a shock to find it now among hardheaded secularists! If religion must live in a post Copernican, Darwinian, Marxian, Freudian, Einsteinian world, then modern secular humanism lives in a world that has seen Auschwitz, Hiroshima, Babi Yar, Sharpeville, Selma, Detroit, and Watts — to name only the most obvious cases. This is no century in which to appeal to the natural goodness of man.

Perhaps the veneer of American civilization is momentarily thick enough to contain the fantastic forces that crouch at the door of consciousness, waiting to turn men into beasts. The future looks less sanguine. What the civilization is producing en masse today is the savvy cynic whose wisdom is privatism. He knows the social order can't be beat, that it gives minimal returns for exorbitant demands. He knows that most people, despite their surface friendliness, are out to use him and he, to survive, unfortunately must do the same to most of them, so he withdraws from social concern. He hopes more modestly now to find a few people to love and thus give his life some sense of worth and value. Yet every such relationship, he soon discovers, requires a sacrifice of freedom and an assumption of responsibility greater than any society demands. A reasonable man concludes that he had better find such pleasure as he can, particularly if he can do so without undertaking too many obligations. That is the attraction of marihuana. It promises instant, autonomous satisfaction as LSD purports to give ecstasy reliably. The flower people rationalize the escape of drugs as a higher morality. Less radically, the surfer, alone and free, at one with wave and sun, is the other symbolic figure of the younger generation.

For the truth seems to be that if the current secularity is not substantially diverted, it will create a new paganism. Outwardly, modern men are enlightened, sophisticated. Existentially they show the same despair that the ancients had of human destiny. Once again man stands helpless before great, external forces he cannot seem to understand or master. Once again his life becomes a pattern of propitiation and evasion, a desperate hope of salvaging something before the black doom descends. In pagan man, classic or contemporary, there is little hope for moral passion, for the essence of Biblical righteousness is the rejection of the apparent in the name of the ideal, the transformation of what seems to be in the light of what ought to be. With man's sense of transcendent reality gone, limited to the amoral realism of what is, secularity becomes triumphant in paganism and the ethical fervor of the prophets becomes a miracle if not madness.

That is what makes the current moral emptiness of philosophy so tragic. No thinker or school of thought stands against the gathering forces of paganism to proclaim the fundamental human importance of the ethical. Once secularity might claim as its own either natural or moral law theories of philosophical ethics. Now, despite occasional backward looks born of mounting desperation, modern rationality rejects both, probably because it realizes that the one implies natural theology, the other the God required by practical reason. So ethical speculation today concentrates on the logical structure and appropriate entailments of given varieties of ethical statements. That is indeed helpful to know. However, it tells men nothing of where ethical statements will come from or why, with the full authority of secular rationality, people should care about them.

Such hope as there is for conscience in the secular world arises among those who have come to know in their very being that nothing is more important than persons. This commitment to single selves has no general philosophy to substantiate it. Those who hold it would, as a matter of fact, probably be highly suspicious of any such theory as ideology. Believing persons are important, they distrust all structures, philosophical or social. That is why they rush to protest when institutions which should be concerned with persons, such as the government or the university, seem to deprive some men of their rights. Then they protest by personal means, by themselves going to sit, stand, sing, pray, read, or simply be there. Their means is consistent with their concern. That is their power. So even when their themes seem foolish and their forms childish, religious men should recognize them as near brothers. The conformists are compounding evil's effect by accepting it as natural. At least the protesters know that men must work to transform their lives in terms of a transcendent vision or they have as good as lost their humanity.

This vision of the worth of the individual man has great ethical, revolutionary potential. Its power has been felt in the struggle for civil rights and its healthy radicalism continues to manifest itself in the growing recognition of the antipersonal thrust of this civilization.

Yet even this one spark of secular conscience must be analyzed

in terms of religion's hard-won sense of social realism. True, the
commitment to persons might power a mighty secular ethic, but
can it, as long as it remains secular, ever be strongly enough
rooted to have any significant impact on the incredibly powerful
impersonal forces ranged against it? This society is not merely
apersonal in tendency. Technology, its supreme glory and strength,
makes it determinedly antipersonal. Technology means abstrac-
tion, generalization, repetition, mass — and it means power, incredible power for those who control its techniques. Place the
awesome power of modern technology behind all the impersonal
social and intellectual forces that surround man and the hope
that persons will long seem important is unrealistic. To defy this
overwhelming might, hopefully to shift its direction, it is not
enough to have a modest conscience of convenience, some general forms a few intellectuals follow, an occasional spasm of the
will or even a strong personal inclination. What humanity needs
now is not merely morality but moral stamina, moral fiber, moral
endurance. To be useful today conscience must be tough enough
to stand up to the incredible energies regularly brought to bear
against it. It must be committed enough to work for goals that
demand great effort and greater patience. It must be determined
enough to bear suffering and setback and yet refuse the ultimate
victory to amoral realism.

Only such a conscience is worthy of the name in the real
world, and secular institutions show no promise of producing it.
Even the concern for persons felt by the minority on the college
campus is not likely to endure long unless it is grounded in a
transcendent standard. For why, in strict, hardheaded secularity,
should men care and work for others? If we are honest, most of
us know ourselves to be as deceitful as we are trustworthy, as
hostile as we are loving, as destructive as we are creative, as self-
serving as we are righteous. We often question why we should
accept ourselves as worthwhile and we are right — unless we know
that there is that beyond us which accepts and affirms us as
persons, unless there is a God who testifies by his Covenant
presence with us that we are, even in all our conflict and division,

supremely of worth. And why should we, the strong and competent, the successful and the powerful, fully give of what we have won to the weak and the bumbling, the uninteresting and the unattractive, the failures who make up the bulk of society? Why really should the powerless, the widow, the stranger, the orphan, be the test of our humanity? It is only if we acknowledge that the rights of men are not derived from what they seem to be or seem able to produce, only if we confess that our worth is intimately linked to theirs by our both being grounded in one transcendent source of value. Then we understand why we must love all other men even as we come to understand why we must love ourselves. Then we will know no human task is more important than brother love regardless of temporary outcomes.

There will be no moral stamina without moral ultimacy and no moral ultimacy without a transcendent moral ground.

This is what religion uniquely has to offer in an emerging technological, pagan civilization: a sense of perspective that will power and sustain man's ethical life, a knowledge of and faith in that transcendent God who demands nothing before righteousness to men, and who demands nothing less than a society holy as he is holy.

Such trust made manifest will, at the minimal level, and with apologies for the flippancy, at least serve to keep the secularists honest.

For a generation or so now they have prided themselves, especially in the Jewish community, as being more ethical than the religiously observant and by this righteousness justified their denial of their roots. Today, the values of their pious forebears are eroded and the secular world gives them increasingly little nourishment for their idealism. If they insist on playing " ethicaler than thou," then religion would have reason to pursue its sense of God's moral demands if only to challenge the secularists with how little they are really doing and how much they ought to do. That is what the rabbis knew as a controversy for the sake of heaven.

Positively, and more seriously, religion remains the one hope

for creating a sizable enough minority of men to keep a technological society moral. It can do so not by avidly compromising
with the secular understanding of existence but precisely by affirming its faith in a transcendent order of being that grounds and
guides man, yet gives him his freedom and demands that he use
it for ethical ends.

Today's believers may be poor in piety but insofar as they remain religious they know they affirm a transcendent God. That
explains why, as suddenly as it blew up, the "death of God"
movement has collapsed. It obviously had nothing to say to secular men who had all along known there was no God. When it
spoke to religious men, when it called for "death of God" theology, religion without transcendence puffed itself out on the
question of human value. When Altizer specified that his vision
of the death of God meant moral nihilism and that this black
night ought to be joyously welcomed; when Hamilton refuted all
the humanist transformations of Christian ethics and in his own
denial of God could come up with nothing better than Jesus as
guide though not ideal; when Rabbi Rubenstein in outrage against
Auschwitz gave up all of the transcendent God except the Holy
Nothing but then could not explain why in accord with its amoral
nature men should not be bestial to one another — then all but
a few academicians withdrew from it. Contemporary believers
may not know much about the nature of God and even less
about the proper logical form for intelligible statements about
his transcendent reality, still they seem to know, particularly if
they have loyalty to the Jewish tradition, that God and human
values cannot be separated. They find themselves unable to give
up God if that entails surrendering the ultimate significance of
the ethical task. That intuition, that ethics, has a transcendent
source, that the transcendent stands over against us at least in
moral confrontation, still glimmers in the darkness of many a
modern heart. Religion can perform no more important task today than to keep it alive.

It can do so in four ways. The first of these is the prophetic
act. Here by dramatic proclamation or deed, it takes its stand

over against the society and calls it to account. How can religion say it serves a transcendent, holy God if knowing him it yet acquiesces to the injustices that men continually do to one another? Religious institutions and theoreticians must learn to lead in this process of speaking out, for they have a moral perspective which is becoming increasingly rare. Their unique social stance imposes upon them a unique social responsibility.

Yet the word cannot exhaust the prophetic task. In large part that is because society has stripped even the best of human words of their meaning. In part, too, it is because religion has often seemed to think it could discharge its ethical obligations by preaching, another word fallen into disfavor. By not following speech with deed, or, better, by failing to speak most loudly through its deeds, religion has left the entrenched sinfulness of society substantially untouched. This is not to argue that consequences are the measure of significant religious action. It is only to say what every man knows from everyday life, that talk is cheap where values are concerned and action very precious. The purpose of acts is to testify more loudly than words can as to what really counts. Knowing what the silence and passivity of apparently well-intentioned men made possible in Germany, these are today mortal sins, as they should have been since the days of Leviticus and its injunction about standing silently by our brother's blood. Moreover, action sometimes changes things, as the civil rights struggle has demonstrated, though it has not changed enough.

Yet the involvement in the cause of civil rights was not unequivocal. Some religious men have become so enamored of its demonstrations that they have found them to be the one sure instrumentality of God's working in contemporary history. For them the mass protest has become the paradigm of religious action, civic agitation the most significant form of prophetic religion. In Judaism's appreciation of the prophets, even of Eldad and Medad, it never concluded that the essence of continuing religiosity could be prophetic speech or actions. Instead, it knew that the dramatic and exceptional find their proper historic expression in the continual and the disciplined. Stamina, endurance, fiber — that is history's test of morality. Prophecy is the privilege of the few but history is the province of the many. Religion may gain vision from prophecy; it changes history by mass discipline, by halachah, the religious structuring of everyday existence.

The second way, then, in which religion carries out the work of conscience in our time is to sensitize people to the ethical deed and habituate them to practice it. Thus, in the civil rights struggle the major positive thrust has gone from demonstrations to the creation of halachah, for example, tutoring — though demonstrations are often, obviously, still necessary and riots will undoubtedly recur as frustration continues. Tutoring is less dramatic and satisfying, more time-consuming and personally demanding than agitation. However, now that prophecy has done a great measure of its work, tutoring, housing, education, jobs, and day-to-day self-respect and hope will mean more. Religious men need continually to find and cultivate such halachic expressions of the ethical, acts that in their depth and continuity both testify to the reality of belief and change social reality in terms of it.

Religion enters a realm of great danger as, prophetically or in discipline, it becomes involved in specific issues. Its humble competence is with the ground and goal of conscience. As it moves from the transcendent to the political it inevitably becomes less expert until in its nitty-gritty involvements it may altogether lose sight of its commanding Lord. Yet what good is it to hear God calling men to do justice and love mercy if they do not seek to do it in the real world? The Bible is not a record of men who were religious in the abstract or played it safe for God's sake. It is precisely the story of real men trying to serve the real God in the only place where it really counts, in real history. So religious men of conscience will sometimes make mistakes. Or they may conflict with one another as they seek to apply what seems to be the same religious understanding to the same problem. Or they will discover that they have nothing new to add to what secular technicians have already suggested in a given problem area. Now the religious perspective seems to be superfluous if not complicating. Yet even though it cannot be unequivocally applied, the truth of the previous analysis stands. Motivation remains critical and stamina decisive. If the humane continues to shrivel in our society, religion's transcendent view is not only indispensable, it might even be made a source of unique practical suggestions.

There is, however, no way of determining in advance the single best means of socially implementing the religious dream. When religionists diverge on concrete issues, the least their common belief makes possible is a clarification of why they differ. In such an analysis the different hierarchies of value or the estimates of the situations stand revealed. That process itself may often lead to more unified action. In any case, men may then judge more clearly what beliefs lead to one course of action or the other. In clarifying the choice before them, in helping them decide what they really believe, even such religious differences will be a significant means of increasing responsible human living.

Yet something further must be said about the risks of involvement. For the foreseeable future there is far greater peril before God in not taking a stand than in taking what may later prove to have been a foolish one. If religion, out of self-seeking or self-doubt does not sound the alarm, there are fewer and fewer moral guardians to do so. Better a false one from time to time in the name of zealousness than a record of safe accomplishment compiled at the cost of collusion with sinfulness. What is more tragic than a watchman become an accomplice in crime?

It also seems reasonably clear, again for the foreseeable future, that when in doubt, religious men should cast their lot with the prophets and criticize the *status quo*. It has always been easy to give in to the powers that be. The emoluments are gratifying, the results of criticizing painful. But religion cannot be satisfied with society as it is if God's will is its standard. The best of secular welfare states is not yet his Kingdom. Loyalty to transcendence means dissatisfaction with the present.

All of this life of conscience then, religion's role, the prophetic act, the disciplined existence, the assumption of risk, stems from a relationship with God. Surely that is so obvious it should be no surprise, yet it directs us to two other levels of religious action related to the pursuit of conscience. Both seek to keep men more conscious of God, particularly in his transcendent holiness.

The first of these is the religious duty to study. That is not a privilege for academicians or a luxury for gentlemen scholars but a commandment for everyone who would be a man of conscience. The frantic pace and intricate involvements of modern life bind people to this time and place, dimming their ethical perspective. Study of a religious tradition gives men breadth and distance. Through it they live in other ages, climates, economies, governments. They see the human problems and the divine imperatives recapitulate themselves in ever-changing ways. They watch the people of Israel find and be found of God, and struggle to take him seriously. They learn with the prophets what it is to see God in politics and to stand against kings and populace in his behalf. They experience with the unbroken chain of rabbinic interpretations what it means to try to apply God's law to human lives in ever-changing circumstances. Such study may not give them specific answers to air pollution and nuclear proliferation, but it can give a sense of what God has perennially required of men — better, of who he is — that will help lift men above the transient as they move to take their risk-filled stand.

Yet it can often give specific guidance as well. True, the social situation of modern man is substantially different from that of the past, yet the human condition is radically the same. Seen through the eyes of three thousand years or more of the Torah tradition, many a new social problem looks familiar, many a contemporary human situation is not really unique. As today's Jews clarify what they still share with their spiritual forefathers they will better be able to be guided by an abiding faith in meeting their challenges rather than be misled by a social fad.

Finally, nothing ultimately arouses and sustains the sense of the transcendent as does liturgy. In the hundred blessings Judaism requires every day, in the formal stated prayers of morning and evening, each individual man and the community reach out to renew the reality of their relationship with God. Prayer hardly seems relevant to social action. Religious activists often complain about pietism when there is so much work to do in the world. Perhaps religion was too quiescent in the past and what it needs most today is a somewhat reckless pursuit of ethical adventure. But men dare not lose sight of the God who commands them. Beyond today's high cause waits tomorrow's routine. Religiosity is tested by boredom as well as by sacrifice. If conscience means stamina, the transcendent God needs to be sought regularly. Men need him for forgiveness as much as for courage, since they can rarely be certain that they are doing God's work rather than their own sinful work.

The final truth is that one cannot rip the pursuit of conscience out of the integrated religious life. Prayer and study find their relevance in witness and discipline. They in turn find their ground through the inner religious life, and both modes need communal reinforcement as well as personal participation. Of course, modern man and his sick society need a new sense of conscience. Yet what they need more fundamentally is a rebirth of Biblical religion. Over the centuries, despite all its failings, religion has remained true to its moral mission. In that effort it has shown itself capable of surviving the most unbelievable human barbarities, the most destructive stretches of despair. Despite everything, it has ever again raised up that critical minority of men who have refused to let mankind forget the God of transcendent holiness. That is what it needs most critically to continue to do today.

PART
IV

JUDAISM AND CHRISTIANITY

Chapter

12

CHRIST–KILLERS NO MORE

My father's formal Jewish education in the small Polish town in which he grew up included nothing directly related to Christianity. He learned his Hebrew alphabet, read his prayer book in Hebrew, and worked at translating the weekly portion of the Torah and the Prophets together with the traditional commentaries. Had he continued his studies or been a phenomenal student in those years before emigrating to America, he would have studied the Talmud and Jewish codes. Had he covered enough of these materials, he might have found some references to Christianity, but he would not have come across anything directly treating of the councils of the church, their creeds, dogmas, or decrees.

His informal Jewish education was far more effective than what he learned from books and teachers: it was unforgettable. He still remembers being taken by his mother into a basement and hidden there for two or three days while a pogrom raged outside. That traumatic experience or the possibility of it lurked in all the quiet references a growing boy heard about non-Jews and their attitudes toward Jews. How could his understanding of himself as a Jew not be shaped substantially by what the majority thought of him? Thus my father's education as a Jew in Europe cannot be understood apart from the education which the non-Jewish community gave him informally but, nonetheless, effectively as to what, in all reality, it means to be a Jew.

My formal childhood Jewish education took place in a congregational school in Columbus, Ohio. I can recall many of my experiences during those years vividly. The joy of the holiday celebrations, the boredom of the English textbooks, the inadequacy of the instruction, the tedium of studying Hebrew in classes that seemed to make no progress — all remain quite present to me, and incidentally make me wonder how they engendered in me, as they unquestionably did, the desire to learn more about a tradition that must be better, I knew, than the way it had been presented to me. In all those studies, however, which began in early childhood and continued until I graduated from high school, I recall no books or projects dealing with Christianity, Christian doctrine, or the relationship of Judaism to Christianity. To be a Jew, particularly when one lived as a small minority amid so attractive a non-Jewish culture (in those days one could say Christian culture), one had to know Judaism, its laws, its practices, its history. One could gain these essentials without ever discussing Christian doctrine.

My informal Jewish education was undoubtedly highlighted by an incident that occurred on the playground of my elementary school, the Heyl Avenue School. I do not remember the year or the exact sequence of events but I recall the critical details. They concern the usual boisterous, muscular play of boys aged nine or ten and the emergence of tension between me and a friend. One day high spirits led to a confrontation. To silence me for good he flung his vilest epithet, " Christ-killer." Someone started the fight — I hope it was I — and there was a black eye and tears. I do not remember whether I thought then that he or I had won. Now I know that in such a fight, while one may retain one's dignity, everyone loses. We never fought again; no incident nearly as physical ever recurred in my several brushes with anti-Semitism; and while I have forgotten much of the anguish of that moment and many of the details, I have not forgotten the event itself. What it did to set the quiet apprehensions and wariness of the

non-Jew that were the dominant attitudes of my newly accli-
mating, immigrant Jewish community may be easily imagined.

My daughters in their religious education in a predominantly
non-Jewish suburb of New York have learned far more about
Christianity in their synagogue school than did either my father
or I. Their textbooks, some of which I helped prepare and edit,
contain specific references to Christianity, particularly as it arose
from Judaism and as it affected Jewish life in the Middle Ages.
When they are older, they will probably spend a year studying
other religions and use the pioneer Jewish textbook in this field
by Miller and Schwartzman. I had the great joy of reviewing the
chapters of that volume which treat of Roman Catholicism with
Father Gerard Sloyan and the chapters on Protestant Christianity
with Dr. John Bennett. Our Reform Jewish Commission on Jewish Education could not be content to publish something descriptive of their faith which in all good conscience they could not
say was reasonably accurate, though, of course, we made our own
Jewish evaluation of it. I have no reason to believe that there is
anything in that volume or the other texts my children have
studied which will need revision since the Second Vatican Council, though some additional material on the mood of the Roman
Catholic Church today would be desirable.

The informal education of my daughters offers much more room
for change and improvement, not that my wife and I, or our
Jewish friends, or our Jewish community have inculcated such
negative attitudes toward Christians that, due to the action of
Vatican II, some substantial compensatory change is in order. If
anything, I think that over the years we have gone far out of our
way to cultivate respect and understanding, not only for our
Christian neighbors but for all men in a world of " united nations." (If we worry about our teaching concerning other faiths,
therefore, it is rather that we have made our children so open-
minded that they may believe we think it makes no difference
what one believes and, more specifically, whom one marries!)

However, we are not the only educators of our children. One
day as I was planting in our garden I heard a conversation be-

tween my two eldest daughters and one of their friends from up
the street. They were playing on the swing set some distance
away. Although I did not catch every word and could not go closer
without making them self-conscious, I heard enough. My girls
were then, I think, seven and five. Their friend was six and had
just finished her first few weeks in the local Roman Catholic
parochial school. She asked in all friendliness why my girls had
" killed God." The phrase was so incomprehensible to my little
ones that their first level of retort was that they hadn't killed God
but had found him, since the Jews gave one God to the world.
When the interreligious semantic confusion was cleared and Jesus
became the topic of discussion, my girls insisted that the Romans
had done it — though where they had learned this with the oldest
only in the second grade I still have no idea. That historical assertion brought the discussion to a stalemate. The girls continued
to play while I made my way to a chair to consider the mysteries
of Jewish existence.

Since that day neither of the girls involved has ever mentioned
the incident. Should they read this account, I sincerely doubt
that they would recall its having taken place. That evening at
dinner, however, they both asked me numerous questions about
the death of Jesus, and my wife, whom I had told of the discussion, and I exchanged several significant glances during the
conversation. I do not know whether they have ever run into any
such overt anti-Semitic incident since that day. They have certainly never mentioned any to me. Although they have been welcomed in their overwhelmingly Christian schools, girl scout troops,
and neighborhood, they have also been taught a certain sense of
limit, a certain realistic definition of what it means, socially, to
be a Jew. In their continuing education about their Jewishness
who can judge how determinative that incident on the swings
will prove to be?

I have permitted myself these personal references because I believe they illustrate quite concretely the hopefulness and the
problems of Jewish-Christian relations over the past few generations and particularly their existential reality.

For the Jew of the United States, anti-Semitism has been a changing phenomenon and one that has, with some setbacks, steadily changed for the better. What was in my father's generation a matter of life and death had become in my childhood an occasional blow and to my daughters a series of remarks. Today sociologists regularly report that most American Jewish adolescents cannot recall ever having experienced anti-Semitism. With the economic experience and social openness of the post World War II era, anti-Semitism has become increasingly less manifest, but only the few would go so far as to say it does not remain potent if latent. It should also be added that since we American Jews are all the children of immigrants give or take a few generations, we somewhere must recall that had not some forebear had the courage to trek across the ocean and were democracy not the incredibly magnificent achievement it is, we too might have been Hitler's victims. The outer, growing security plus the decreasing inner apprehension as the non-Jewish world makes its professed democracy more real — these shape the reality of Jewish living today.

If we inquire how Vatican II may have an effect on Jewish-Christian relations, we can answer quickly. Formally, it will have none. The decrees on revelation, the liturgy, the laity, seminary education, the church, are of little concern to Judaism. The decree on non-Christian religions will call for little change in Jewish texts or teaching. Jewish children still need to know, among many positive things in Jewish history, the tragic facts of murder, pillage, segregation, and inquisition which mark the relation of Christians with Jews until modern times and without which modern anti-Semitism for all its nonreligious character is inexplicable. To be sure, the schools should be expected to indicate that in the late twentieth century the Roman Catholic Church indicated that anti-Semitism is incompatible with its doctrine, properly understood, but that is no reason for removing from the textbooks what is, on the whole, an unhysterical, even gentle treatment of those ancient, sad days. (The thirties gave rise to a continuing cry in the Jewish community that children should

not be traumatized in their Jewish education by being exposed
too much to the suffering of Jewish history. The textbooks and
the tone of Jewish educational materials still reflect this roseate
view to such an extent that how to teach children about the
holocaust under Hitler has become a major methodological problem.)

The critical question, then, is how the Council's decrees and
mood will affect the informal education of Jews, that is to say,
that unplanned and unprogrammed but very definite introduction
to the nature of Jewish identity which the non-Jewish world gives
the Jew, thereby substantially affecting his self-image as a Jew.
How can anyone hope to know the answer to that question? Surely
there are grounds for faith that what was swept through much of
the church on the highest level will one day reach into most
parishes and their institutions, if not in the remaining years of my
daughters' youth then in their children's lives. When one realizes
what the past ten years have done to transform what once seemed
like an immovable, or paralyzed institution, then there may be
some confidence that the next ten years will see conciliar decrees
become personal deeds.

But there must be doubt as well as to how much the old traditions of Christian anti-Semitism can be overcome. The very
fact that the Jews are included in a document dealing with all
non-Christian religions seems to show little appreciation of the
uniqueness of the Children of Israel as the recipient and bearer
of God's revelation in history. If it is explained that the document
does indeed take cognizance of this uniqueness but it was more
politic in the working out of the Council documents to include
the Jews here, then it is just those politics which give one pause
in agreeing that this matter has been settled once and for all as
definitive doctrine. The decree does not say so but it is clear that
the church is remorseful at what befell the Jews in recent decades
and, therefore, for all the sorry history of medieval times which
led up to it. For that sentiment and goodwill one must be grateful. Yet this era of good feeling gives rise to the nagging possibility urged on by the experience of two millennia (with the last

thirty years the worst) that this document is therefore only the expression of the spirit of this chastened age and that the now latent anti-Semitism of Christianity may yet reassert itself.

Let me adduce another personal experience to illustrate this Jewish ambivalence. It derives from one of the most profoundly moving ecumenical experiences I have had, the Catholic-Jewish Colloquy that took place at St. Vincent's Archabbey, Latrobe, Pennsylvania. When one of our sessions was ended early so that the Catholics present could attend a special Mass, several of us expressed interest in attending and were invited to do so. The Mass, the first I had attended that used English, was a breathtaking experience. The congregation, about two hundred seminarians, sang many of the responses in antiphony to a choir, both groups using music composed by members of the Abbey. In contrast to the static Masses I had attended or seen before, this was a dynamic service with constant interaction of priest, choir, and congregation, of Latin and English, of movement, sign, and silence. How familiar to the Jewish heart was the recurring psalm " It is good to give thanks to the Lord " (*"Tov l'hodot ladonai."*)! Even the Gospel reading of the day struck a special echo in the Jewish ear: " Think not that I have come to abolish the law and the prophets; I have not come to abolish them but to fulfill them. . . . Whoever relaxes one of the least of these commandments and teaches men so, shall be called least in the kingdom of heaven; but he who does them and teaches them will be called great in the kingdom of heaven." [1] The evident piety and devotion of the men participating in this service could not fail to stir those of us who were merely observers.

Yet all this warmly felt appreciation could not overcome another emotion. This Mass was in celebration of the saint's day of John Chrysostom. The great Jewish student of the church fathers, Louis Ginzberg, wrote of him: " His sermons . . . *Adversus Judaeos* . . . mark a turning point in anti-Jewish polemics. While up to that time the Church aspired merely to attack the dogmas of the Jews . . . with Chrysostom there began the endeavor which eventually brought so much suffering upon the Jews, to prejudice the whole of Christendom against the latter, and to erect hitherto unknown barriers between Jews and Christians." [2] Malcolm Hay, who goes on to quote some of the saint's utterances, says of him, " The violence of the language used by St. John Chrysostom in his homilies against the Jews has never been exceeded by any preacher whose sermons have been recorded." [3]

Perhaps while rejoicing in the sainthood of Chrysostom the church can surmount his attitude toward the Jews. Although rabbis do not normally have the rank of saints, there are numerous rabbinic utterances that Judaism would not identify with its noblest doctrine. Yet John Chrysostom illustrates well the question that the future poses, Who speaks truly for the church? More important, what will the future acts of Roman Catholics, and the Protestants who have been influenced by the Second Vatican Council, teach the Jews? That is hardly a question for a Jew to answer but only, with some hope, to wait and see.

NOTES: *Chapter 12*

1. Matt. 5:17-19, quoted here from the RSV. The Abbey was using an early, experimental version of the new confraternity translation.

2. *The Jewish Encyclopedia,* Vol. IV, p. 75, art. "Chrysostomus Joannes."

3. Malcolm Hay, *The Foot of Pride* (Beacon Press, Inc., 1950), p. 27.

Chapter

13

ON THEOLOGICAL DIALOGUE
WITH CHRISTIANS

The critical issue concerning Jewish-Christian dialogue is not whether it shall be but only what kind it shall be. The world has anticipated any theoretical discussion of the issue. It is busily at work forcing men in a dozen different ways to confront their neighbors of many climates and states as well as faiths. If Jewish thinkers choose not to engage in dialogue or to show how it ought most usefully to be conducted, Jews and Christians will not remain blissfully ignorant of its possibilities. Our society in its mindless mixture of exploitation and chance will teach them what an informed leadership might have hoped to guide to responsible goals.

Religious men of both faiths should have a special interest in this new world become a neighborhood. Morally, we must confess that a good deal of the prejudice that separates man from man, nation from nation, race from race, has been empowered by religion even where prejudice has not arisen in its midst. For that prophetic judgment we must be grateful to those secular critics who, judging us by our own standards, have called us hypocrites. Such prejudice cannot be ended merely by giving people facts, for its roots lie beyond the rational. Yet the word " Jew " will sound differently when Christians know the countless lives of sanctity created by post-Biblical Judaism, and the term *goy* will lose its repulsiveness when Jews know what the Mass and the

cross and the creeds represent. The very fact that one faith deems
other faiths worthy of serious brotherly concern will itself help
to make dialogue more than superficially effective.

Yet the most positive reason for interfaith conversation is that
the search for brothers should always be a primary task of those
who wait for the coming of God's Kingdom. We do not stand
and serve alone. God knows all men as his covenant with Noah
and his sons makes clear. As our individual religious communions
sustain the individual, so the knowledge that other religious communities stand alongside ours in the night of history should give
us all added hope as we seek to survive in faithfulness.

These truths, and others, can hardly be gainsaid. That is why
they may be stated with such brevity. What keeps Jews and
Christians both from applying them in their institutions is not the
falsity of the ideas but our fear. We are afraid that if we affirm
that which we mutually believe, we shall lose our individual faith.
That dread is particularly great within the Jewish community. In
the century and a half that Jews have been coming out of the
ghetto they have seen how social integration leads to religious
defection. If the rate of conversions to Christianity has not been
high in recent years it is only because religion is out of style and
ethical secularism a far more attractive because a less identifiable
option. With society so seductive, shall a minority faith concern
itself about dialogue with other faiths? It hardly has the energy
to transmit to its own people an introductory understanding of
its view of man and God and history. After centuries of Christian
persecution climaxed by the Nazi horrors (which Christianity may
not have caused but for which it provided the background and
against which it did not vigorously protest) how can one say it is
important for Jews to learn about Christian belief?

These special Jewish fears are widespread among believing, car-
ing Jews. They must not be repressed among Jews or in discussion with non-Jews. They must be stated. What makes Jewish-
Christian discussion possible today is that such candor and
honesty in speaking of one's fears is welcomed and appreciated.
So the very negative statement itself, predicated as it is on some

men's willingness to listen to another man speak his heart's pain is not the end of dialogue but its beginning. To know one is welcome to acknowledge his apprehensions to men who genuinely care is already to initiate the process and transform the broken past in a slight but significant way.

These diverse tensions explain the strange paradox of Jewish attitudes toward discussions with Christians. There is virtual unanimity in the Jewish community that in matters of social welfare Jews should welcome opportunities to work together with Christian groups. Wherever education, race relations, poverty, health, the aged, the handicapped, world peace, and other such issues are at stake Jews should not hesitate, but rather make a positive effort to join interfaith programs that will call attention to the evils and seek to remedy them. Moreover, this is a Jewish religious obligation and therefore it will not do to have the Jews represented by secular agencies but only by the religious organizations — congregational, educational, or rabbinic.

There is little question, too, as to how such interfaith activity should be carried out. A generation ago Jews were so eager to speak to Christians that they snatched at every chance to be seen together. Today the emphasis is on mature self-respect. Jews may be willing to engage in dialogue, even to initiate some programs for it. They are, however, no longer willing to be perpetual initiators of such talks or the major financiers of projects to encourage them. Once interfaith activity was often the only Jewish concern of the Jewish participants. Now it is clear that Judaism can only be properly represented by those who believe it, know it, and practice it. Jewish faith must be the foundation of any significant contact with Christianity. That being so, it is clear such extra-communal concerns are not primary to Jewish existence, though they have a legitimate if secondary claim upon the believing Jew. Thus the insecurity that leads either to total withdrawal or to fawning and obsequiousness is no longer acceptable. A mature democracy makes it possible for a self-respecting Judaism to cooperate with an interested Christianity in a way that can serve only to benefit them and their society.

That positive attitude toward dialogue does not, however, carry over into the realm of theology. There a substantial difference of opinion divides thoughtful men in the Jewish community, and these differences, while largely following Orthodox versus non-Orthodox lines, does to some extent cut across the denominations. Yet even here some areas of almost universal agreement remain. What is not debated is the need to study and understand contemporary Christian theology. That activity, it is conceded, may teach Jews much today, whether by disagreement or concurrence, even as it did in the classic periods of Jewish philosophy. Here, too, the security of contemporary Jewish belief as over against the blandishments of contemporary intellectual movements asserts itself. There is no longer a great fear of such ideas or systems sweeping Jews from their faith by the power of their modernity. Thoughtful Jews have seen these intellectual fashions come and go so frequently in recent generations and have learned enough about the lasting truth of Judaism, even in its modern dress, not to fear confronting the best that modern Christianity has to offer, or to refuse to learn what it might have to teach.

What is being argued in the Jewish community is whether Jews ought to participate in face-to-face discussions of theology with Christians. Four major reasons have been advanced against such exchanges. Since Christianity is now past its historic peak and is no longer the controlling spiritual power of our civilization, Jews need not concern themselves with it on a practical level. Psychologically, Christianity is too intimately involved in Jewish minds with the guilt of the holocaust for Jews to be able to speak or listen freely to it, and the silence of organized Christianity during the Six-Day Arab-Israeli War has only increased those emotional barriers. Humanly, it is not reasonable to be expected to participate in a conversation with someone whose only interest is in converting you to his faith. Theoretically, religious faith is so private a matter that it cannot meaningfully be conducted between faiths.

All these contentions contain some measure of truth, yet I do not find them persuasive either individually or collectively. Rather, it seems to me that together with the insights that they offer there is a good deal in them that is at best shortsighted and at worst immoral.

To call this a post-Christian age does not mean that Christianity has lost all influence on our civilization. It remains the single most important nongovernmental institution known to Western man. It shapes much of the thinking and the lives of the tens of millions of its adherents and by its very presence in the culture exerts a powerful effect on the admittedly substantial minority of those who are not its members. To say that Western culture is becoming increasingly secular is not thereby to say that Christianity is dead. Much of the good inherent in contemporary secularity derives from the Christian civilization that gave rise to it. Without it where will modern secularity find the basis for a strong ethical or culturally humanistic drive?

At the fall 1966 Harvard Divinity School Jewish-Christian Colloquium many Jewish speakers in the discussion group on Torah and dogma seemed to find it some indication of the truth of Judaism that ours had become a post-Christian era. In my remarks then I termed this attitude " Jewish triumphalism," and events since then have confirmed the accuracy of that term. After centuries of hearing Christianity laud itself over Judaism because of its numbers and power, Jewish resentment has finally found a decisive response. In preferring secularity to Chistianity, the world seems now to have learned what loyal Jews always knew, that Christianity is not true enough. The next implication would seem to be that Judaism, having said so for two thousand years, is thereby justified and validated. Such notions say more about the psychology of their proponents than about cultural or theological realities.

Should Judaism, as a matter of deliberate policy, prefer men to be secular rather than Christian? That might be the case if with typical nineteenth-century optimism it might be assumed that educated, enlightened men will be ethical, perhaps even religious in a general sort of way. Surely it is difficult for a son of the prophets to have such trust in contemporary secularity. It is one thing to appreciate an anti-Puritanism that leads to a more natural acceptance of pleasure. It is quite another to see it become the new life principle that self-gratification is the primary goal of existence and fun the measure of how alive one is. The old Protestant ethos may have known too much of restraint but to turn Christian freedom into modern anarchy, to create an ethical mood whose only barrier to action is " why not? " is to set loose a new possibility of immorality that can only appall those who love the Bible. Jean-Paul Sartre points the way. Freedom is the only good and to choose freely the only virtue, regardless of the content. What atheist existentialism expounds affluence empowers in a post-Christian era. Can any spokesman concerned for Jewish authenticity welcome the new immoralism which this has begun to bring into the Jewish community? Is a post-Christian culture that teaches Jews the secular virtues of sensual indulgence and living for themselves in the present a social context Judaism should welcome? It is naïve to think that secularism without the Bible will somehow be Christianity without Christ or the church, that it will be, so to speak, closer to Judaism than Christianity is. The more realistic view would seem to be that a secularism unguided by Christianity and paying no attention to its handful of believing Jews, would become a new paganism, one far more dangerous than anything the prophets and rabbis ever fought against. With its idols internalized and pandering to every creaturely need of man to keep him productive, that new paganism, in its sophistication and immediate appeal will make Judaism appear to be irrational self-denial, a masochism swathed in illusion. Already secularism's power makes itself felt. Jews no longer convert to Christianity. Why take on even its burdens? Rather, they drift into the new secularism and except for the tiniest minority, they are not even distinguished by a strong ethical impulse as was the old socialist or liberal substitute faith. When they make a commitment to the good life, they are speaking in terms of personal pleasure not of moral service.

If that is the drift of a post-Christian era, then Judaism and Christianity are at least united in having a common enemy. Judaism has far more in common with Christianity than with a secularism going pagan. That is not meant as a denial of the real and disturbing differences between the two faiths. Much critical remains to be said about the concept of a Judeo-Christian tradition (though Jewish triumphalism often asserts itself in such discussions). Yet with all such qualifications one cannot assert that it makes as much sense to speak of a Judeo-Greek or a Judeo-Roman tradition as a Judeo-Christian one. There are unquestioned fundamental similarities in these two faiths. They may not be so evident when they are compared to each other but they emerge quite clearly when the contrast is to an unbelieving, unethical cultural style. Judaism needs Christianity as its ally against the paganization of our civilization unless it prefers to withdraw to a self-imposed ghetto or quixotically try to do the job alone. Realistically, then, theological dialogue is necessary to determine to what extent Judaism and Christianity can be partners in this critical social enterprise.

That is a relatively pure motive for talking to Christians about theology, yet there is a parallel matter whose overtones are less noble. It has to do with the strange discontinuity in discussion as one moves from matters of social welfare to theology. In the former case, Jews are eager to speak and work together with Christians. In the latter they fall silent and withdraw. Is that a reasonable condition to put upon such a relationship? Can people really expect men to work intimately with them in areas of vital human concern and yet refuse to speak to them, politely to be sure, when they inquire about one's values or commitments? The anomaly is made all the more pointed because Jewish participation in intergroup activities, it has been demanded, ought to take place only under religious auspices. How, then, can one close off in advance inquiries about what faith grounds Jewish concerns in an area of social action or what beliefs guide them in taking a given stand on a certain issue?

The suspicion cannot be repressed that Jews advocating such a schizophrenic relationship to Christians are less concerned to work together as human beings than to use Christians for Jewish social ends. Where the issues immediately affect the Jewish community as in fair employment practices or ending university restrictions, the Jewish gain is clear. But even in such apparently disinterested matters as race and poverty it is obvious that any right secured for minorities below the Jews in the American status scale makes the position of Jews that much more secure. But Jews have nothing to gain, they believe, from theological dialogue, so they will not talk. If Jews come to issues of social ethics only as another power bloc interested in alliances with those who share their power aims, then they should say so. To mask such motives with the ideology of interreligious cooperation is intolerable. If the basis for joining together in the activity is religious, then it should be discussible.

To say that one simply cannot talk to Christians on the level of faith because of the anti-Semitism necessarily inherent in Christianity or more specifically because of its inevitable association with the holocaust does not mitigate the charge of exploiting interfaith social activities. If every Christian is potentially a Nazi or has the shadow of a Nazi about him, how can one in all integrity join him in social ethical projects? To do so, if that is one's experience or belief, would be the height of hypocrisy. That is not only a reason to break off theological discussion face to face but to withdraw from contacts of every kind with Christians. Surely for those who have been indelibly scarred by the Hitler fury that would be understandable. Yet that has not been the decision of the majority of those who came through the holocaust and for the overwhelming majority of Jews brought up in America. The word *goy* has lost much of its ancient bitterness. A phobia toward Christians and Christianity seems more pathological than the virulent hatred it sees behind every Gentile face.

The silence of the Christian organizations during the June 1967 Arab-Israeli War seemed to many to provide some support for the previous argument. When there was a Jewish crisis of the first magnitude, when American Jews needed the support and help of the churches and church bodies, it was not forthcoming. The silence was damning, and official statements after the war, calling for the Israelis to surrender Old Jerusalem or the West Bank have only made matters worse. American Jewish sentiments run high on this issue. That is precisely why it is desirable to apply as much rational analysis to it as possible.

Perhaps the first thing to do is to put what happened in perspective. Individual Christians were not silent during the first few days of the war. It was quite clear that the sympathy of most American non-Jews was with the Israelis and they did not hesitate to say so to almost any Jews whom they recognized. Many a highly placed Christian clergyman was heard from, often without being asked, and in the weeks after the closing of the Strait of Tiran and before the war, certain Christian bodies did call for justice for the State of Israel. One cannot then equate being Christian with being against the State of Israel. More important, specifying that it was the institutional church, not all individual churchmen or most church members, which was most grievously absent, should refute the more critical assertion: anti-Israelism is only the new form of traditional Christian anti-Semitism. That is simply not true as individual Christian attitudes have demonstrated. The position taken by the official bodies is less likely the result of some residue of ancient Christian anti-Jewish phobia than of the special concerns of institutional Christianity as contrasted to individual Christians. That would seem logical unless one assumes that any person who takes a stand against the State of Israel in a critical matter is *ipso facto* an anti-Semite. Some Jews feel that way and it makes no difference to them whether the critic is Jewish or Christian. He is to them, a Jew-hater. But no believing Jew can place a political entity, even a Jewish one, beyond all judgment. One wonders what such nationalists would have said to the prophets. To the Jewish heart there may have been little ambiguity in the recent Arab-Israeli war. Only to a jingo could there have been none. Yet if some twinge of doubt about the war could agitate even those who love the State of Israel, surely it is possible for those whose loyalties are not primarily concerned with the Jewish people to confront the same ambiguous proposition and decide against the State of Israel. For myself, I believe that almost any man of reason and morality could have seen the necessity of Israel's fight against the Arabs and should have championed her cause. Yet I can understand how some men of reason and morality might disagree. There are surely anti-Semites who have condemned the Israelis for winning and refusing to give back what they have won until a cease-fire becomes a formal peace. Their voices are heard in respectable journals and in respected institutions. However, not every man who argues against the State of Israel is sick on the subject of Jews. The institutional church has a hierarchy of value different from that of most American Jews or most individual Christians on this matter. Where the one gives the highest priority to Jewish survival and the other high value to Israeli forbearance and democratic accomplishment, church bodies have their responsibilities to Christian Arabs and their hope of converting the remaining Arabs. United States support for the State of Israel identifies Christianity with Israeli interests in Arab eyes and makes the possibilities of conversion that much more difficult. The churches may be concerned about Jews and anxious to right ancient wrongs. They are more concerned with their Christian Arab brothers and their mission to convert the world to Christianity. That is not hatred of the Jews, even indirectly. It is a scale of value which, when applied to an ambiguous situation, might well make possible a decision that would prefer silence to pro-Israeli declarations. I think that decision was wrong, by my standards even immoral, but I do not think it was pathological. It disturbs the free flow of conversation as any great difference of opinion will. It does not prove that conversation is impossible or undesirable.

How odd it is to hear Jews charge that if Christian groups do not support Jewish interests in critical matters, Jews should not engage in theological dialogue with them! It comes with incredibly poor grace from the lips of those who have righteously insisted that dialogue is impossible with Christians, since they are only interested in converting Jews. Now the truth appears. These Jews are only interested in dialogue if they convert Christians to positions valued by the Jewish community! Surely any discussion entered

with only one possible outcome is necessarily ugly and objection-
able. That is not to say participants in dialogue should not want
to change each other's point of view. There is little sense in talking unless you believe what you are saying and want the other person to see the truth of your view. What is unseemly is to insist
that if he does not agree, it was not worth talking, or to listen to
what he says only as a pretext for pressing one's own view. Obviously, Christianity desires the conversion of the Jews in a way that
Judaism does not reciprocate. Yet insofar as many modern Christian theologians and some churches influenced by them have seen
such conversion of the Jews as an eschatological rather than a contemporary matter, a task more for the Second Coming than for
the church today, there is a new openness possible from the Christian side in such discussions. From the Jewish point of view, the
very failure of organized Christianity to understand how peoplehood is a theological category to Jews and how the State of Israel
becomes a concern of Jewish faith is precisely a reason to intensify
theological discussion, not to end it. That does not mean Christians will always thereafter agree with Jews but only that in their
new moments of decision they may understand the Jews and Judaism as they understand themselves.

Can such conversations be at all significant if religious faith is
at its heart so private and personal a matter as modern men have
come to know it to be? How can there be a meaningful exchange
when what is at stake is simply unutterable? Surely no man can
tell another the fullness of the truth his heart has come to know.
That is not a Jewish truth but a modern existentialist dictum. It is
as well known to Christians as to Jews, if not better. Hence there
can be no illusion on either side that any such discussion can present all that either faith holds dear. Rather, each tradition knows
that in its own midst there are areas where communication ceases
and privacy must rule. How much more will that be true between
different religions! That is agreed. Now, however, the real question
can be raised. Since not everything can be said, is there nothing at
all worth saying? That hardly seems the case. In the first place it is
clear that saying faith is ultimately too personal for utterance is al-

ready to communicate something about it. Faith is not beyond all meaningful statement. That is not a philosophic quibble, for there are practical consequences to the ability to say something about one's faith. One studies one's own traditions about it because one knows they can help one in a way one often cannot help oneself. One speaks with the men of one's community to understand what is common and what is individual in one's affirmations and is thereby enriched. One can learn from the books of other faiths something about one's own. In the case of converts one can know enough of what they have come to learn and believe of Jewish faith that they can responsibly accept it. Only because it is reasonably clear that they affirm it in their private way with sufficient authenticity may they be accepted in the congregation of Israel. These things are all possible and real in the realm of what can be said about faith. They explain why theological dialogue may hope to accomplish much in an exchange between faiths even though they must stay within the bonds of finitude.

That theoretical issue is surely less the real Jewish objection to theological dialogue than is the fear of the loss of identity. Such interfaith discussion seems to imply, certainly at the early stages of acquaintance, an emphasis on what the faiths have in common. Perhaps that stage of naïve brotherhood is already past in the contemporary level of dialogue. Still, the fear of similarities persists. When Jews and Christians learn what they have in common, will it still be possible for Judaism to remain its unique self? Does not the very act of interfaith discussion place a higher value on what the faiths share rather than on that in which they differ? Surely that seems to be the attitude of the average American. He democratically assumes that what all faiths affirm is superior to what any one faith holds alone. That is why it is not so much God as organized religion that is at death's door in our society.

This problem of individuality amid sameness plagues our civilization as a whole. Similarity is the key to our planning and production, our organization and facilitation. How, then, shall we be persons, individuals, single selves?

Neither conformity nor rebellion solves the problem. The former is sinful because it demands that we surrender our peculiar selfhood, the one thing which makes us *us*. Beatnik rebellion is no more successful a strategy. Bare feet and dirty long hair may make us look different. They do not guarantee that we are ourselves rather than the slaves of middle-class conformism in transformation reaction. Maturity will not be found in either total immersion in the life of mass man or external assertions of one's difference from others. We become ourselves only when, knowing we are like all other men, we simultaneously acknowledge what distinguishes us from them. As the Talmud puts it: "When a king of flesh and blood stamps his likeness upon coins, they are identical, but when the Holy One Blessed Be He puts His image on all men, each comes out unique."

It should also be a major concern of theological dialogue that in the regard for what is shared in common the differences are equally made manifest, that in learning where the faiths stand together they come to understand better where they must stand apart. The most important thing we can do, then, is to create a polemics of dialogue.

This proposal will sound strange to those for whom ecumenicity is the emotional opposite of the attitudes implied in the older practice of polemics. They have meant enmity, harshness, the total negation of the antagonist's position. They breathed an air of total deprecation and complete disparagement. They assumed the polarization of the debaters with one possessing God's own truth and the other necessarily damned in God's own eyes. Is not the general appreciation of dialogue precisely the death of the old polemical style? Instead of seeing the agents of the devil, men now can see persons of another mind; instead of the damned there is only the different; and both sides now stand open to the beliefs that they share.

The progress is morally unmistakable, yet it has not been completed. It is easy to be friendly when men agree. It is therefore more important for the relations between them to see how one is prepared to accept the other's difference, his rejection of one's fundamental faith, his negation of what one considers to be the saving truth. Difference is the test of religious goodwill; the ability to create a meaningful polemics will be the sign of ecumenical good faith.

Obviously these modern discussions should not be the old type of interfaith warfare, yet they should retain something of its search for ultimacy. The difficulty of the old polemics was their premise that man could give God's judgment on other men's faith in the here and now of history, often to the point of having sword and fire enforce that decision. How easily, then, could the will to power, personal or social, appear to be the will of God and texts become pretexts!

These procedures might have been justified then in Christian-Jewish polemics by the belief that in Sacred Scripture both sides had a public, absolute standard of theological right and wrong. Today, with some exceptions, we do not believe religious truth is adequately transmitted in such objective fashion. The Scripture may be said less to specify religious truth than to point to it in a uniquely significant way. Judaism and Christianity can still hope to find public agreement in the text, but only insofar as they agree to study it in terms that historians think may disclose what it once meant. If they seek to discuss what it means in truth now, then they do not read the same text in the same way. When we talk of the nature of our faith today, even if we use texts to found and justify our belief, we know we have references ultimately to a personal realm. That is why our polemics can have a new tone. The public, open, common knowledge of that truth, the other man's full recognition of our right, cannot be required or compelled now, in finite history. He may not know it because we cannot fully convey it or he may, in fact, know it as well but as inexpressibly as we do. In God's good time, the messianic time, we shall jointly see the earth " filled with the knowledge of the Lord as the waters cover the sea." Until then we must be committed to theological pluralism, to the finitude of our own understanding as compared with God's, to the possibility that the other man may have as much of His truth as we do.

The polemics of dialogue are new by virtue of being conducted in such a sense of humility. Yet they should nonetheless search for the truth that is inherent in what divides the faiths. That is what makes them polemical, for we shall undoubtedly discover that we are as fundamentally committed to what separates us as to what unites us. Christians may find that a faith in the Christ brings their various churches a unity more fundamental than their different doctrines of the church would seem to imply. Yet faith in the Christ divides the Christian and the Jew, and insofar as he is understood to be a person of the Trinity, that divisiveness will affect the underlying sense of unity which Jew and Christian might find in the unity the Jews understand the Biblical God to be. Here the differences seem to be decisive for the entire structure of the faith and almost more fundamental than the similarities. What began, then, as a search for distinctiveness in unity, may well eventuate in a statement of what to each is a more adequate faith than the other has. Description gives way to evaluation and commitment. With ultimate truth at stake in difference, these researches in confrontation are the modern, existential version of polemics.

Yet if all faith is ultimately subjective, why undertake to probe these differences? Since they cannot ever be fully explained, we expose ourselves to the charge of avoiding brotherhood for emotional or ethnic or other morally insubstantial reasons. That should serve as a warning that this effort may often end in frustration and misunderstanding. Yet the opposite danger is greater. Not to try to clarify the areas of disagreement is to imply that differences are not significant at all. It is to permit a shallow relativism to dominate religious discussions or to prevent them from taking place at all. What can be said about our faith should be said in order that we may exercise such checks and balances upon it as we are capable of. In that way we shall be most responsible in believing. In the secondary process of trying to speak of our differences to men of another faith we may better learn what it is that we have been trying to say to ourselves, perhaps as we hear it from the other or recognize in his fallacy or distortion what we did not mean.

We can likewise be enriched by the nonverbal as well. How true it is that one understands a faith better by knowing its believers than by reading its theoreticians! The faithful convey something beyond words of its style, its feel, its effective nuance. This is as critical to understanding its validity as its ideas, if not more so. Hence we must stand in polemic-over-againstness not just to the minds of men of other faiths but to their faith-full lives as well.

That is where the real issue of conversion arises. We confront the adherent of another faith in the full human dimension of the truth on which he stakes his existence. If he does any less, if he does not really believe, if his faith is an intellectual game, his practice and stance an unmeant routine, he is not worth speaking to on these matters. If he is fully present in his faith, his authenticity makes its demands upon us. Simply being there, he challenges us to accept his saving truth for ourselves. We cannot deny him that right without asking him to sacrifice himself as self. To engage in this sort of polemic, then, must mean to hold oneself open to the demand made by the other's very person, that we accept his truth. The risk of dialogue, even polemical dialogue, is conversion. But it applies to him as to us. He must be as open to us and our truth as we are required to be to him. He must be as willing to risk what may happen when we talk as we are, and neither of us must in all good conscience exert any influence upon the other to make a decision other than what logic permits between minds and respect between persons.

The risk of conversion is worth taking for those who seek the truth passionately and are reasonably secure in the road that they have thus far come, for the customary alternate to such conversion is a new and fundamental self-affirmation. To know in the depths of one's being that the other's truth is not one's own generally means to be sent back to one's own truth with some new insight into its nature. That may, at best, be an existential variety of negative theology, yet it is also true that negation is one of the classic means of definition. In knowing who we are not, in having some intellectual and personal sense of why we are not sharers in other faiths, we become more fundamentally rooted in our own. That is not an easy or a troubleless path, but compared to the slander and hatred of other faiths into which religious groups have regularly allowed themselves to be drawn, it is one far more worthy of our God.

What an extraordinary contribution religion could make to the contemporary world if it could show men how to understand one another in their differences! What vulgar sinfulness infects every level of our social relations when we must deride and defame those who differ from us in order to affirm our own worth! It is but one step from this hatred of the different to its destruction. Does not the Bible itself remind us that the first religious polemic, one over the nature of sacrifices, ended in Cain's murder of Abel? The time is ripe, as it always has been, to learn that lesson. We are all of us sons of Adam, though some of us still till the fields while others tend the flocks. Whose sacrifice the Lord will in due course accept he alone can fully know. Until then we shall serve him best in being ourselves, not in trying to become our brothers, in accepting our brother for what he is, even where he is not like us, and thereby accepting ourselves as well in all our distinctiveness.